Praise for #MoneyChat
THE BOOK

"For years Dorethia Kelly has been a valuable financial expert in the community helping numerous clients achieve financial success and overflow. Finally...she has made her expertise and knowledge available in print. Kudos for #MoneyChat THE BOOK. Now consumers have a user-friendly, practical, and much needed guide with simple steps to get out of debt and become financially independent."

—Glinda Bridgforth, author of *Girl, Get Your Money Straight!, Girl, Get Your Credit Straight!* and co-author of *Girl, Make Your Money Grow!*

"If you are tired of people simply telling you to manage your money better, but not telling you how, this book is for you. Dorethia has provided realistic methods for getting out of debt and preparing for the financial life you want now!"

—Ryan C. Mack, author of *Living in the Village, Build Your Financial Future and Strengthen Your Community*

"Searching for a great long-term investment? Look no further than Dorethia Kelly's new book #MoneyChat. Spend a few hours curled up with this financial guide and you will reap dividends for years to come as you learn how to get out of debt, set yourself up on solid financial ground, and prudently invest your money for your future."

—Manisha Thakor, co-author of *On My Own Two-Feet and Get Financially Naked*

#MoneyChat

Contact information for Felicity Media Group, LLC—www.dorethiakelly.com/felicity

ISBN: 978-0-9863383-1-1 (paperback)
ISBN: 978-0-9863383-2-8 (ebook)

Library of Congress Control Number:

Ordering Information:
Special discounts are available on quantity purchases by corporations, associations, and others. For details, contact www.dorethiakelly.com/felicity

Cover photo by Robin Gamble

#MoneyChat

HOW TO GET OUT OF DEBT, MANAGE YOUR MONEY, AND CREATE FINANCIAL FREEDOM

DORETHIA KELLY, MBA

Dedication

For my children and grandchildren,
my prayer is that you always have financial success.

To my mother, I love you, that is all.

To my husband Will, it's primetime, who knew? Love you.

How People are Rockin' Their #MoneyChat!

Although I earned a great income, I was never really able to save money. After working with Dorethia, I was able to see where my money was going and create a realistic financial plan that I could follow.

—S. Johnson, Administrative Assistant, Washington, D.C.

Working with Dorethia was very eye opening. As she helped us match our behaviors and spending habits with the numbers, we realized unexpected expenses were stopping us from reaching our goals. We developed a fund for those irregular expenses are now better able to forecast throughout the year and add to savings.

—The Cordaways, New Haven, Connecticut

Dorethia helped me understand the mindset of paying myself first and how it was transferrable across several goals. I began to set aside a percentage of my paycheck not only for emergency savings, but also when I needed to prepare for a large purchase. This allowed me to save and pay cash for a previously owned vehicle as opposed to financing a new vehicle.

—L. Corbin, Healthcare Professional, Detroit, Michigan

An Important Message from Dorethia

I REALIZE THERE'S A LOT to cover, so before you begin reading, definitely download these bonus materials. They are free to everyone who has purchased this book.

If you haven't purchased, well what are you waiting for? LOL! Grab your copy here and you'll be sent all the bonuses listed on the page: **dorethiakelly. com/moneychatbook**.

If you have purchased go to **dorethiakelly.com/moneychathub** and get all the additional resources that are mentioned throughout the chapters.

xoxo,
Your Financial Coach,

Contents

Section Three
Growing Your Money

Section Four
SECURING YOUR MONEY

Your Next Steps

#MoneyChat: Changing What You SAY and DO With Your Money!

WATCH YOUR MOUTH! HOW MANY of us heard that as kids? Both of my hands are raised, my mouth was always getting me in trouble. Whenever you hear yourself saying something negative about your money, tell yourself to WATCH YOUR MOUTH.

I have always believed that our words have power, if you are constantly speaking the problem, you won't be able to achieve your goals. Negative words put us in a bad mood and do more to discourage us from moving forward!

I can remember, in my early 20s, never really hearing anyone say anything positive when it came to money. Someone was always moaning about not having it, needing to borrow it or loaning it out but never getting it back. They couldn't pay bills, debt collectors were always calling—they just stayed stressed out about debt and never having enough money. I began to take on that mindset, and started complaining about how little I had, or always complaining about being broke.

One day, I just got tired of listening to myself. I kept thinking, *There HAS to be a better way.* I was determined not to live my life moaning and complaining about not having money. So, I set out to teach myself about money management, increase my skills so I could make more money and teach my girls how to live a financially free life.

I began to read everything I could about money management, I watched YouTube shows, read blogs, listened to podcasts, and attended webinars. I was so excited about what I was learning because it was foreign to me. For once I was creating a PLAN for my finances and it felt good! So good, I wanted to help the world learn it too. I began telling my friends, family, coworkers, acquaintances—anyone who would listen! Well, some listened, some ran the other way, lol.

This is how #MoneyChat came to be, I wanted to change the conversation around money, so habits could change. I wanted to make it not so intimidating and erase the shame of past mistakes. #MoneyChat is about what you SAY and DO with your money, it's about lifting up those around you by sharing positive financial habits. It's about community and encouragement.

Maybe your story is different, maybe you always had enough like some of my clients. So much so that you felt like it didn't matter what you spent, there was always more where that came from. Some have never heard the word NO, so there are no boundaries, no discipline, no financial planning for the future—just a lot of spending.

It doesn't matter which end of the spectrum you are on, creating a roadmap for your money doesn't mean deprivation, in fact, it's the exact opposite. When you are intentional about where it's going, you put yourself in a position to be able to buy what you want. When you've covered your bills, saved some, gave some, invested some and planned for goals or fun spending, there's nothing left to want.

Dump the Guilt + Shame

"Sure, you wish you did some things differently. But there is no sense in becoming burdened with regret over things you have no power to change."
—Rihanna

We've all made some mistakes with money. Whether it's as simple as not keeping track to making constant poor decisions. What I don't want you to do is beat yourself up. Reading this book proves that you are making a step forward. To rehash every mistake you made in your mind or in conversations is a waste.

I realize that you may have some major stuff going on that is really stressing you out. I've been there, I too had to remind myself to stop speaking the negative. Even if it's true. This doesn't help you fix the situation, so why not focus on what does?

You are not the only one who has ever faced your issue. Remember there is nothing new under the sun but the players of the game. I don't say this to diminish its impact, but so you know you aren't alone.

So, let's dump the guilt and shame and move forward one step at a time. Give yourself some time and some grace. The #MoneyChat Fam is a community of everyday people just like you on the path to financial freedom. We've got your back!

The #MoneyChat movement is about changing what you say about money so your actions will follow! We call it "Rockin' Your #MoneyChat!" In my financial coaching practice, there are four recurring things people want to do:

1. Get out of the debt hole

2. Learn how to manage their money

3. Grow their money by investing and saving for retirement

4. How to protect what they've worked so hard for

Many just don't know how to make that happen, they know that they should do these things, but don't have the steps to take. I wanted to write a book that holds their hands so to speak. Don't just tell me what to do, give me the tools.

There are a couple of other topics that are crippling millions of families but aren't discussed as much—IRS debt and gambling. Don't think big time casino ballers gambling their fortunes, but the middle-class families with a loved one blowing their paychecks.

At the foundation of changing your financial future, is building an emergency fund. In this chapter I share my experience and how you can start an emergency fund, bit by bit—even when money is tight.

I believe in progress, so throughout each chapter in this book, I've included an action for you to take. It makes no sense to simply read what to do and not have some accountability. In my financial and business coaching practice I always give homework so each chapter gives you an 'assignment' as well.

Look for **'DO THIS'**

at the end of each chapter. Underneath your assignment, you'll find your #MoneyChat Mantras to say each day, remember, our words have power!

Please share your success stories with me at **hey@dorethiakelly.com** and connect on social:

instagram.com/dorethiakelly   tiktok.com/@dorethiakelly

youtube.com/dorethiakelly   linkedin.com/in/dorethiakelly/

Here's to ROCKIN' YOUR #MoneyChat!

xoxo,

SECTION ONE

Getting Out of the Hole

CHAPTER ONE

Don't Manage Your Debt—Get Rid of It!

#MoneyChat

"Rather go to bed without dinner than to rise in debt."
—Benjamin Franklin

I HEAR A LOT ABOUT debt management and it makes me cringe. It just seems that if you are only trying to "manage" your debt, you will always have debt. So, there needs to be a disclaimer. Yes, you need to manage your debt *but* with the end goal of getting rid of it.

- Managing debt means paying creditors on time, watching your credit score, and not incurring any new debt.

- Getting rid of debt includes all of these, plus making extra payments to pay it down faster until it's gone. That is the only way to get out of the hole, paying more than is due.

Getting out of debt takes discipline. I know, we've all heard that before, right? Some joke about it: *I'll never get out of debt, I like having a new car every three years, I love to shop too much, it's the only way I can go on vacation*—you fill in the blank. All these excuses stem from not wanting to make the sacrifice and do the work required to live life differently, to save for the "fun" stuff as opposed to borrowing for it.

Though it may not be easy, the payoff is peace of mind along with more money to spend, save and invest. Got it? Good! Now, let's get to the nitty-gritty!

Get Organized

Who do you owe?

Find those old notices, pull out those shoeboxes, sift through your emails and look in those junk drawers. It's time to face the music.

List the debts you know of and get a copy of your credit report to see what may be outstanding that you've forgotten about.

List all your debts—even the ones you aren't currently paying.

- Creditor
  Who do you owe?

- Purpose
  Why do you have this debt? What did you use it for?

- Interest rate

How much does it cost you to borrow?

- Balance
  If you were to pay the debt off today, how much would you need?

- Monthly payment
  How much is due each month?

- Due date
  What day is the monthly payment due?

You can track this information in a list like the one below.

Creditor	Purpose	Balance/ Payoff Amount	Interest Rate	Monthly Payment	Due Date
Credit Card	Build Credit	$8,601	21%	$150	15th
Car Co.	Car Payment	$7,232	15%	$346	1st
Furniture Store	Living Room	$1,500	15%	$175	30th

What I like about writing it out like this, especially listing the purpose, is that it allows you to face yourself and your habits with debt head on. In the example above, it says the purpose of the Capital One Credit Card was to build credit. The strategy is to get a credit card, make a purchase and pay it off each month. It is really a strategy for people who are financially stable but want to up their credit score. As you can see, this cardholder did not follow through as planned and ended up in a lot of debt. Defeating the purpose, right? RIGHT! Hopefully never again.

Negotiating With Creditors

You want to deal directly with creditors so try to make arrangements with them before they send your debt to a collection agency that will add on their fee for you to pay as well. Once you and the creditor have agreed on a monthly payment or a payoff arrangement, get that agreement in writing before you send your payment. Also, do not give creditors your bank account information or allow them to automatically withdraw from your account. I got burned once because I gave a creditor my bank account information. Instead of taking the agreed upon amount, they took the entire balance due! When I cried foul, the rude account representative replied, "So what? Sue us!" From then on, I sent electronic payments via online banking.

If your payments have been late or you haven't been paying at all, you may not be able to negotiate a lower interest rate or payment. But if you have a lump sum of money, you will most likely be able to strike a deal. Creditors would rather get some of their money than none at all.

CREDIT CARDS

If you are in good standing with your credit cards and your score has improved or remained solid, you can contact your lender and ask for a lower rate or shift your card to a 0% interest rate card.

Pay It Off!

Once you've made your list and have completed your negotiations, it's time to start paying your debt off. I'm a fan of the Debt Snowball Method of debt elimination because I know it works. With this method, you pay your debts from the smallest to the largest, in that order, regardless of interest rate. Why the smallest debt first? Well, because you gain some traction and a sense of accomplishment as you pay off each one. It feels better to knock off three debts at $250 each than to start chipping away at $10,000 right off the bat.

I've used the Debt Snowball Method to pay off a significant amount of debt myself. Over the years, I've shown my clients this simple process and those who use it have paid off a ton of debt. I don't believe in reinventing the wheel. I just find what works and do it. Simple as that!

How the Debt Snowball Method works:

	A. DENTIST BILL		B. CREDIT CARD		C. CAR PAYMENT	
	Amt. Owed	Mnthly Pmt	Amt. Owed	Mnthly Pmt	Amt. Owed	Mnthly Pmt
Month 1	280	50	1,700	100	12,000	350
Month 2	230	50	1,600	100	11,650	350
Month 3	180	50	1,500	100	11,300	350
Month 4	130	50	1,400	100	10,950	350
Month 5	80	50	1,300	100	10,600	350
Month 6: Paid Off A. Dentist Bill	30	30	1,200	100	10,250	350
Month 7			1,100	150	9,900	350
Month 8			950	150	9,550	350
Month 9			800	150	9,200	350
Month 10			650	150	8,850	350
Month 11			500	150	8,500	350
Month 12			350	150	8,150	350

Now use $50 from A to help pay off B faster

	A. DENTIST BILL		B. CREDIT CARD		C. CAR PAYMENT	
	Amt. Owed	Mnthly Pmt	Amt. Owed	Mnthly Pmt	Amt. Owed	Mnthly Pmt
Month 13			200	150	7,800	350
Month 14: Paid Off B. Credit Card!			50	50	7,450	350
Month 15					7,100	500
Month 16					6,600	500
Month 17					6,100	500
Month 18					5,600	500
Month 19					5,100	500
Month 20					4,600	500
					4,100	500

Now use $150 from B to help pay off C faster and so on until you are debt free

Note: When listing your debts, do not include your mortgage

The mortgage isn't included because it is generally one of your largest debts. In certain cases, I also suggest clients place student loans in the same bucket as mortgages. In those instances, you continue to make monthly payments, but tackle their payoff once your other debts have been taken care of. Again, each case is different, there is no cookie cutter solution, this is just a general rule you can follow.

Should I Consolidate My Debt or Use a Credit or Debt Counseling Agency?

Though I don't openly promote these services, I'm not totally against debt consolidation or debt counseling companies, because I realize that everyone is not a do-it-yourselfer. That's like me building a website, I can do it, I have done, but I hate it! However, I do caution people to read the fine print and make sure they're clear on the services being offered and the fees being charged as there are many scams. It's important for you to know that no one can erase your debt or wipe your credit report clean, I don't care how much money you give them. Don't fall for it!

Debt Consolidation

When you consolidate your debts, you are taking out a new loan with a lower interest rate and monthly payment in order to roll several loans into one. Though the new loan will be the same amount, it may extend the life of the individual loans that comprise it because it's considered "new" debt. There are fees associated with debt consolidation but there shouldn't be an "up front" fee. So please read the fine print. Please do not pay someone $400–$1,000 to erase your debt. You will be upset at the end of it.

Credit/Debt Counseling Agencies

A good debt counseling agency not only negotiates with your creditors, but it also provides education and solutions to help improve how clients manage money in the future. There may be a startup fee, but it should be under $50. Your monthly fee may be around $20–$50. The debtor (you) sends one lump sum payment to the counseling agency, which then pays the creditors on the debtor's behalf. Here's the tricky part.

Many people send their money to agencies that aren't reputable, and the creditors never receive any payments. Now the creditors are adding late fees to the debtor's account and sending collection notices, all while the debtor is unaware and out of the money.

How do you find a reputable credit/debt counseling agency?

1.   Look for at least three companies that have been around for a

while—anywhere from five to 10+ years. They will have online reviews from customers that you can use in your decision making. There are websites that will show you a comparison and rating of various agencies.

2. Compare the fees and services each company offers. What will they deliver for you? There are also sites that will show you a comparison of company services.

3. Visit the following websites to find an accredited company:

   a. National Foundation for Credit Counseling (NFCC); **www.nfcc.org**

   b. The Association of Independent Consumer Credit Counseling Agencies (AICCCA); **www.aiccca.org**

 DO THIS **ACTION STEPS**

1. Download your debt snowball template at dorethiakelly.com/moneychathub and list ALL your debts smallest to largest.

2. Make a decision to become debt free. Commit to the journey and determine not to create any new debt.

3. Read Chapters 6-8 thoroughly so you can get your money on solid ground.

 SAY THIS **MONEYCHAT MANTRAS**

“ *I will be debt-free!*

“ *I am the master of my money!*

Robin's Journey to Getting Out of Debt

When I began working with Dorethia, I was at a point in my life when I knew it was time to make a change in my family's finances. I was one of those people who always looked the part; you would never know I was living from paycheck to paycheck. I earned a decent income, but spent it all and then some, relying totally on the next payday. That was normal for me; I didn't see the need to save. People looked at me and thought I had it all together. In reality I was wearing a sharp pair of shoes that I hadn't even paid for yet.

I was very excited to work with Dorethia. I took her suggestions very seriously, except when she said I should do my own hair for a few months. I was used to getting my hair done several times a month. That was a hard pill to swallow, but I eventually came around. I saved over $140 per month to add to our debt payoff. (My weekly visits were $75 each; I cut them down to twice a month.) I began tracking my income and expenses, stopped using credit cards, and ate at home more. I discontinued our cable service, a $125 per month savings, and used that money to build my emergency fund. That was the first step in my coaching process: to create an emergency savings, something I'd **never** had. I began to see results and finally had money at the end of each pay period. No more paycheck to paycheck living. It was a huge relief!

By applying what I learned in our coaching sessions and financial workshops, and by reading financial books, I was able to pay off two credit cards and pay down our other three cards. I stopped leasing vehicles and saved for a down payment on an affordable used car. Thanks to an improved credit score and low interest rate, I was able to buy a new home by putting 20 percent down in cash. Instead of buying new furniture for on 'time' or on credit cards, I paid cash. It took about a year and a half to get there, but oh, it felt good!

I am so excited about this new stage in my life. I've wanted to be debt free for a very long time. Now, it's a real goal I know I can accomplish.

CHAPTER TWO

Crush Your
Student Loan Debt

MoneyChat

"If we command our wealth, we shall be rich and free. If our wealth commands us, we are poor indeed."
—Edmund Burke

ANYONE WHO HAS HAD TO borrow money for school has felt the weight of it when it was time to pay up. The student loan debt crisis is hitting Black families even harder. According to a Brookings study, Black graduates are more likely to default on loans than white graduates. And after four years, almost 50% of Black graduates have a higher federal student loan balance than they did when they graduated.[1] Since student loans are a unique type of debt to manage, I've devoted an entire chapter to explaining student loan debt repayment options.

As of this writing there's continued discussion around student loan forgiveness. To stay up to date on the latest information, bookmark this website and visit often: https://studentaid.gov.

Ways to Manage Your Federal Student Loan Payment

Federal student loans are student loans provided through government programs, and these loans come with certain benefits. Here is a breakdown of the payment options whether you're repaying federal student loans for yourself or a child:

Income-Driven Repayment (IDR) Plans

An income-driven repayment (IDR) plan sets your payment based on your income. There are four income-driven repayment plans:

- Revised Pay as You Earn Repayment Plan (REPAYE)

- Pay As You Earn Repayment Plan (PAYE)

- Income-Based Repayment Plan (IBR)

- Income-Contingent Repayment Plan (ICR)

Each plan has different eligibility and payment requirements, but, in general, they allow you to make payments that are 10% to 20% of your discretionary income.

Deferment

Deferring your student loans gives you a break from payments when times are tight. You may be able to qualify for a deferment if you're facing financial hardship or while you're enrolled in another school program. Interest may or may not accrue during the deferment period depending on the type of loan you have. If interest *does* accrue, you need to be very careful—this causes your student loan balance to skyrocket. I'll explain why in the next section.

Forbearance

Forbearance is similar to deferment: it puts a pause on your payments, but interest **will** accrue on your loan during forbearance regardless of the type of loan you have. Forbearance may be something to consider if you're dealing with health problems or you've lost your job. If you're having trouble making ends meet, applying for forbearance is better than not paying your student loans because defaulting can lead to collections activity and even wage garnishment.[2]

Loan Consolidation

If you have many federal student loans, you may be able to consolidate them under one new loan for easier repayment. The interest on your new loan will be the weighted average interest rate of the loans being consolidated.

Beware of Capitalization

Solutions like deferment and forbearance may come in handy when you're having trouble making payments. But if interest is charged while you're taking a "payment vacation," your debt can quickly spiral out of control. This is because of what's called *capitalization*.[3]

Capital what? What is that? **Capitalization** is when unpaid interest is added to the principal balance of your loan, and then interest is charged on that higher balance. So, if you owe $45,000 and you don't pay $200 in interest charges for the month, it'll be added to your balance, and the next month you would be charged interest on $45,200. See how that can add up very quickly?

If you look at your loan balances and notice you owe exponentially more on your student loan debt today than you did a few years ago, capitalization is likely the culprit. During deferment, forbearance, or under an IDR plan, always try to pay off the monthly interest because it can help you avoid a balance that increases over time.

Student Loan Forgiveness and Discharge Explained

There are a few scenarios where your student loans may be forgiven or discharged. In both situations, you will no longer be responsible for paying back all (or a portion) of the debt.

Loan Forgiveness:

Educators: Teachers who work full-time for five years in a low-income area school may be able to qualify for up to $17,500 in loan forgiveness.[4]

Public Service Loan Forgiveness (PSLF): This is a program that forgives loans for graduates who make 120 eligible student loan payments while working full-time in a public service job, including government and non-profit positions.[5]

When it comes to PSLF, there are many fine print rules you need to follow to ensure your loans actually qualify for forgiveness:

- Only Direct Loans are eligible.

- Federal loans through the Federal Family Education Loan (FFEL) Program and the Federal Perkins Loan (Perkins Loan) Program are not eligible.

But you can make these loans eligible by doing a Direct Loan Consolidation.[6] Keep in mind that **a loan consolidation restarts the payment clock**, so payments you made on the old loans won't count towards your 120 payments. Ouch, right? There's always a trick!

So far, less than 2% of applications for PSLF have been deemed eligible for forgiveness, according to Federal Student Aid data.[7] The most common reason for PSLF application denial is:

1. Not having enough payments,

2. Having an ineligible type of loan, and

3. Missing information.

If you plan to have your loans erased by forgiveness, you must read the rules, double-check that your payments qualify, and reach out to your loan servicer when you have questions.

Loan Discharge

A loan discharge also means you're no longer on the hook to repay your student loans, but for a different reason.[8] Discharge can happen if the school you attended commits fraud in some way, or a life-changing event occurs that makes you no longer able to pay. In unique circumstances, student loans may be discharged in bankruptcy. You can learn more about the eligibility criteria for student loan forgiveness and loan discharge at **StudentAid.gov**.

How Do Private Loans Fall Into the Mix?

Often students have to apply for private loans to continue their education when they have exhausted the allowed amount they can borrow in federal funds. Another scenario is that they didn't qualify for federal student aid and needed to turn to alternative lenders.

These loans typically do not have borrower benefits like federal student loans; however, some private lenders do offer forbearance under certain occasions. If you have private student loans and you can't make payments, call your lender! They may be able to help you avoid default.

Should You Refinance Your Student Loans?

If you're trying to lower your private student loan payment, student loan refinancing is one possible way to do it. Refinancing is when you pay off your existing loan with another one that has better loan terms. Here are the pros and cons of refinancing:

PROS	CONS
Lower Interest Rate Depending on your credit, you may be able to qualify for an interest rate lower than your existing loans, which can save you money	**Credit matters** You typically need to have a score that's at least in the "good" range of 700–750 (FICO) to qualify for the best interest rates on a refinance loan
Lower payment You may be able to qualify for a loan that has a monthly payment that's less than what you currently pay	**Potentially longer loan term** The lower monthly payment on your refinance loan could be due to the stretching out of the loan term. You could pay less per month but more overall because interest will add up over a longer period
Can put loans in your child's name If you took out parent PLUS loans for your child, the child could apply for a refinance loan under their name	**Loss of benefits** If you refinance federal student loans into a private, your loans will no longer have federal student benefits like deferment, forbearance, and income-driven repayment plans. That said, the private lender may also offer a version of these programs

Why Student Loans Should Be a Top Priority

It's easy to say, "I'll deal with that later," but your student loans shouldn't take a backseat forever. The moment you sign on the dotted line you should have a plan for paying it back—early. When you do begin to pay it back, you won't want to only do the minimum balance, but as much as you can to get it paid off fast. High student loan balances can become a thorn in your side as the years go on when you want or need to do other things with your money.

Loans that stick around year after year can make it harder for you to save for your child's education, make major purchases, travel, and live financially free.

Here are a few tips to help you tackle your balances:

- ⊘ **Don't hide from your debt:** Continuously applying for deferment and forbearance can cause your debt to balloon, so face your debt. Pull out all of your statements and commit to making at least the interest payments to keep your debt under control.

- ⊘ **Double up:** Consider making payments twice per month on payday. Automate this payment, so you don't see or miss the money leaving your account. This is where you get ahead to paying it off. If you can't double the payment, add as much as you can—even an extra $20 toward principal is helpful.

- ⊘ **Live light:** Make budget cuts where you can and think about making a few short-term sacrifices. Perhaps you could get a roommate or rent out your place and live with family to keep costs low. There's no shame in doing what you need to do for a few months or years to get rid of those loans!

⊘ **Take on side work:** There may be only so many budget cuts you can make before you need to earn more income. Consider asking for more hours at work, getting a part time job or taking on a side hustle to devote more money to repaying debt.

 DO THIS **ACTION STEPS**

Repaying student loan debt is a journey. Don't get discouraged if you can't pay off your student loans in record speed—it's not a race! Work at your own pace. Be sure to contact your loan servicer if you run into trouble. It's better to be proactive than miss payments because a default on your record can negatively impact your credit.

1. **Pull out your statements.** Follow the same debt steps from Chapter 1 to see where you stand. Write down the loan servicer, interest rate, balance, monthly payment, and due date.

2. **Get help if you need it.** If you're struggling to make payments, consider getting on an income-driven repayment plan. Explore deferment or forbearance as temporary solutions if you need to take a break from payments to get on solid ground.

3. **Research forgiveness opportunities.** If you work in a government job or public service job that may qualify you for Public Service Loan Forgiveness, check to see if your student loans are eligible and speak with your employer to see if your job qualifies. Don't bank on this but check into your options.

4. **Revisit your budget.** Find places where you can squeeze money from your budget to put more funds toward student loan debt. (Definitely read chapter 6!)

SAY THIS #MONEYCHAT MANTRA

" *Student loan debt will not cripple my financial goals*

" *I will create and follow an achievable plan to pay off my student loans*

CHAPTER THREE

It CAN Wait Until Payday! Cash Advance Loans

#Money Chat

I want to travel the country through underserved areas in a truck with an anti-payday loan message plastered all over it, shouting through a bull horn at the top of my lungs about the dangers of these types of money traps!
—Dorethia Kelly

What is a Payday or Cash Advance Loan?

A payday loan is essentially money borrowed to be repaid when you get your next paycheck. It sounds pretty simple, right?

That is until you find out that these loans charge the highest interest rate of any loan option available, and that payday lenders are highly concentrated in lower income areas. Those two attributes make payday loans predatory and deceptive in nature. Many in these areas flock to payday loan establishments because they can't go to traditional banks to borrow when times get tight. It's understandable—the rent is due, the car breaks down, a sudden illness or other emergency pops up and cash is needed fast. Many of those who use these loans aren't financially savvy and may not understand that the interest rate they are going to pay is unreasonable. All they know is they need the money, and this is the only place they can get it. It is easier than ever to get the money, but not so easy to pay it back.

It is well documented that these loans can end up costing borrowers between 400% and 800% in interest. Yes, you read that right. Enraged yet? Payday lenders dispute this, saying their loans aren't meant to be kept all year so they shouldn't be calculated that way. But the truth of the matter is that many people do end up paying on these loans for one or two years. This is because at least 50% of the people who borrow from payday lenders end up having to roll over, or extend, the loan.

How it works:

1. Borrower's bi-weekly take-home pay is $960

2. Borrower requests a $200 payday loan

3. Payday lender's fee is $30 ($15 per every $100) every 14 days = 15% interest

4. Borrower writes a check or authorizes payday lender to deduct $230 from their account (the amount borrowed + fee) on their next payday

The problem arises when the borrower still can't afford the $230 the next pay period and has to extend/roll over the loan. So, you pay the interest on the loan—$30—and incur another 15% ($30 *more* dollars) because it's going to be another two weeks before you (might) pay back the loan. Now you're looking at paying 30% interest ($60) on a $200 loan.

How the 400%—800% in annual interest is accrued:

1. $15 fee per $100 borrowed = 15% interest or .15

2. .15 x 365 days in a year = 54.75

3. 54.75/14 days = 3.91

4. 3.91 x 100 = 391%

It's easy to see how the interest you pay can increase to between 400% and 800% annually as you borrow more or keep extending the loan. This makes payday loans the worst solution ever for borrowing money.

A payday lender can look really attractive when you're in need. You could be facing a financial emergency that has you overwhelmed, and you may not have the credit to go to a bank or credit union. You probably don't have a home to borrow against and asking friends or family—well, let's just say not this time. So, you may think a payday lender may be your last resort. I still say don't do it. They are predatory in nature, and it is difficult to break the cycle.

Banks Are In on the Game

Banks used to partner with payday loan establishments until it was prohibited by the federal government, due to controversy surrounding payday lenders. But over the past couple of decades, several banks have decided to offer their own form of payday loan. They're called direct deposit advances or checking account advances. While bank fees (at $7.50 to $15.00 per every $100) are generally lower than traditional payday loan fees, they're still really high. The advantage banks have, however, is that customers trust them, see them as more reputable than payday lenders, and are more at ease borrowing from them.

How it works:

1. Bank customers are able to borrow up to $500 in any increment ($5, $20, $50, etc.).

2. The money is direct deposited into the customer's checking account.

3. In 14 days, on the next payday, the loan amount—plus fees—is withdrawn from the borrower's account.

4. If the money is not in the account, the account will be overdrawn and the customer will incur overdraft fees, as well.

While banks may not allow you to extend/roll over your loan like payday lenders, they do allow back-to-back borrowing. That is, customers can pay off one loan and immediately request another. But this can turn into the customer using these loans as a way of life instead of as the emergency fix the industry insists they are meant for. Because the debt continues to grow and the interest continues to build up, the borrower is unable to stabilize his or her finances.

The truth of the matter is that most of the people who use payday-type loans can't afford to. They won't have the money to pay off the loans the next payday or the one after that or the one after that. Hence, the industry rakes in tons of money in fees. This explains why payday lenders continue to pop up in lower income and rural areas, preying on the disadvantaged.

Fortunately, many consumer advocate groups are fighting on behalf of uninformed consumers. As of this writing, 13 states and the District of Columbia have banned the operation of payday loan establishments.

DO THIS Action Steps to Avoid Payday and Direct Deposit Advance Loans

If you can take care of your financial emergency on the next payday, wait until the next payday. Payday loans are marketed all over the Internet and in underserved areas—even rich celebrities promote them! But they're really just a financial trap. Reach out to your creditors. Be honest about your situation and ask for an extension. In my professional opinion, it's better to pay the late fee from your creditor than to end up paying sky-high interest on a payday loan.

1. Contact nonprofit organizations. Reach out to churches and other nonprofits that have emergency assistance programs. You will more than likely receive help with your financial emergency. The Salvation Army's and the United Way's 211 services are great resources.

2. Ask for an advance from your employer. Many employers will make confidential payday advances to their employees—interest free. The amount you are advanced is deducted from your next paycheck.

3. Get a second job. You can work remote or go into work, but your income has to increase at least temporarily to get on solid ground.

NOTE: Remember, if you would be able to repay a payday-type loan on your next payday, then you may as well wait until then. There are also great income-increasing ideas in our chapter on *The Infamous Emergency Fund.*

SAY THIS #MONEYCHAT MANTRA

" *I will not be stressed about my finances*

" *I have enough money to pay all my bills, save and invest*

" *I manage my money well*

The Other Man:
A Payday Loan Horror Story

Michele was feeling financially trapped with no options. Although she and her husband both worked, their income was not always enough to cover everyday expenses and the extras that come with having three children. At the time, payday loan stores were popping up everywhere, and to Michele, they seemed like a way to alleviate some of the pain. She thought she could just repay the loan when she received her next paycheck. In passing, she mentioned it to her husband, who was adamantly against it.

Despite his objections, she decided to go ahead and get a payday loan, which began what she called her "affair with the other man," her secret payday loan sugar daddy. She couldn't see what the harm would be: All she had to do was prove she had a job, and with the next paycheck, pay the loan back, which she did. But, she couldn't stop going. It was like a revolving door that became an addiction whenever she found herself facing financial struggle. For two years, she secretly borrowed without telling her husband.

One day Michele sat down and tallied up the interest she was paying on the loans. That's when the epiphany came: she couldn't believe she had wasted hundreds of dollars in interest, money she needed to take care of her family. On top of that, she felt horrible about keeping this from her husband. She decided to stop her "affair" and get a better handle on her finances.

She began to prioritize spending and got her budget under control. She called creditors to make arrangements (and started honoring them—something she hadn't done in the past). Michele says she became transparent with creditors and told them what she could pay every month. She calls it growing up and not allowing fear and pride to take over. She faced her creditors, stopped letting her bills overtake her and began to see success in her finances.

CHAPTER 4

IRS–Uncle Sam is Not Playing With You!

#MoneyChat

"The IRS! They're like the Mafia. They can take anything they want!"
—Jerry Seinfeld

INTEREST ON IRS DEBT IS *astronomical* and it compounds monthly. Don't listen to the ads that say they can wipe out your IRS debt. Though you can negotiate the penalties, the interest rule is regulated by law. There is nothing any IRS agent—let alone debt elimination company—can do about that. It's best to do whatever it takes to re-align your finances so that you do not owe in the future. In speaking to accountants, one mistake people make often is listening to others' tax situations and applying those solutions to their own circumstances.

You don't really know the other person's entire story and could make things worse by not doing your own research and follow-up.

Some Ways People End Up Owing the IRS

1. **Claiming too many exemptions on your W4, resulting in not having enough taxes taken out of your paycheck:** Yeah, you claimed exempt for years and enjoyed all that extra money that belonged to Uncle Sam. You may fly under the radar for a while but the government's payday is coming. And, trust me, it will be a big one! Okay, to be fair, some of you may not have known, initially, that you weren't having enough taxes deducted from your paychecks. I'll buy that for the first year, but year two, three and four? Uh…NO!

2. **Freelancers and small business owners:** These two categories of taxpayer are responsible for their own taxes but often neglect to send in quarterly or annual payments.

3. **Not filing:** If you don't file, the IRS may file for you. You don't want that. The IRS will only give you the minimum deductions and credits—which works in their favor, not yours. They don't know how much student loan interest you paid, whether you made any charitable donations, how many exemptions you should be allowed, etc. Also, if the IRS files for you, you can't amend your tax return.

Make Arrangements to Pay

The IRS has a surprisingly detailed and clear explanation of their payment options on their website, complete with videos!

Visit **IRS. gov** and click on Payments—but I've given you the quick and dirty version below.

Installment Agreement

When you find out you owe, call the IRS to request an installment agreement. This is most often the best option for those behind in payments. If you owe each year, you have to request a new agreement. You may be able to keep paying the same amount, but you need a new agreement, including the new amount outstanding. There are fees for setting this up. Learn more at IRS.gov when you click on Payments.

Offer in Compromise (OIC)

This is a settlement option where you ask to settle for less than you actually owe. You must apply to be accepted and meet strict guidelines.

From IRS.gov:

- **Lump Sum Cash:** *Submit an initial payment of 20% of the total offer amount with your application. Wait for written acceptance, then pay the remaining balance of the offer in five or fewer payments.*

- **Periodic Payment:** *Submit your initial payment with your application. Continue to pay the remaining balance in monthly installments while the IRS considers your offer. If accepted, continue to pay monthly until it is paid in full.*

Innocent Spouse Relief

If you file your taxes jointly and your spouse owes, you can file "innocent spouse." You'll have to prove you didn't know the taxes were underpaid.

Penalty Abatement

This becomes an option when, essentially, the IRS makes a mistake, such as giving incorrect advice or some other error. In this case, the amount you owe may be reduced.

Bankruptcy

This is a question I hear a lot: "Can I get rid of IRS debt by filing bankruptcy?" The answer is yes and no. There are a lot of rules and stipulations when it comes to being able to discharge your debt in bankruptcy.

The answer is NO if:

- You have current property taxes due within a year. Older property taxes may qualify as well.

- There are tax liens on your property.

- Your tax debt accrued as a result of incorrect tax refunds.

- You've had taxes collected by a third party.

- Tax penalties have accrued within three years prior to your filing for bankruptcy.

The answer is YES* if:

- Your tax return was due at least three years prior to your bankruptcy filing.

- You filed the return at least two years prior to your bankruptcy filing.

- Your taxes were assessed at least 240 days prior to your bankruptcy filing.

- Your debt is not due to tax fraud or tax evasion.

All requirements must be met and the debt may be only partially erased.

And what if you don't make arrangements to pay? Well, this is probably not the best move to make as the IRS has the upper hand. They can:

- Put a lien on your property.

- Garnish your paycheck, social security, retirement benefits or other income.

- Garnish federal and state tax refunds.

- Seize your car, home, or other property.

❓ QUESTION

I haven't filed taxes in the last two years. I'm scared to file now because I know there will be interest and penalties.

Yes, there will be interest and penalties, but it is better to file this year than fall further behind. If you do owe, go ahead and call the IRS to set up an installment agreement with reasonable payments based on your income.

If you are owed a refund, you can collect up to three years' worth. Anything past that is forfeited.

DO THIS ACTION STEPS

1. Increase the withholding on your W4 and/or …

2. Make additional estimated payments. Use an online calculator to determine the amount or do the math yourself.

3. For example, if you owe, on average, $3,000 each year, divide that by 12 and that is the additional amount you need to send the IRS each month or have deducted from your paycheck.

    $3,000/12 = $250 per month

4. IF you DO owe—do not ignore the amounts you owe. Call the IRS immediately and make arrangements to pay. You can also e-file payment arrangement forms when you e-file your taxes. Many ignore the statements, they will wait you out and the moment you least expect, you'll get an empty paycheck because it has been taken. So, don't ignore them, make arrangements.

 ## SAY THIS #MONEYCHAT MANTRAS

" *This too shall pass and I will be stronger on the other side of it.*

" *I will not have to pay taxes every year!*

The IRS had Mr. Thomas by the Throat

Many people owe the IRS. Mr. Thomas owed every year and paid according to his installment agreement. However, he added to that debt each year to the tune of about $20,000 in total. Now, I've seen people with much more IRS debt than that, but $20,000 is still a ton considering what the IRS charges in interest. Mr. Thomas earned about $40,000 more than his base salary by working overtime, but he never adjusted his exemptions or paid additional money each pay to cover the shortfall in the taxes withheld.

The first thing I suggested he do was fire his accountant, which was his wife. Thank goodness she did not get offended. Many people know how to handle the simple things in order to do their own taxes; she did both of their taxes using online software. No big deal, but when someone owes every year, you need an experienced tax professional to look at your tax return and show you how to adjust.

As I stated, the interest on IRS debt is outrageous. To continue to add to the debt amount each year is nuts, especially when you can do something about it. But guess what? Mr. Thomas did not want to adjust. Yep. He would rather owe and pay a ton of interest than miss that money in his paychecks.

Therefore, the second thing we worked on was a mindset shift. I showed him the math and how long-term vs. short-term thinking positively affects your finances. With his IRS debt, he would never get out of the hole if he didn't stop the madness and make sure enough was deducted from his paychecks for taxes going forward. He had to go home and think about it, but at the next session, I convinced him to make the change.

Next, I worked with him on a plan to pay off the debt over a two-year period. We explored making extra payments, cutting back on spending (of course), utilizing future overtime earnings, and selling investments. At the end of the day, he was relieved to have someone hold his hand through the process and tell him what he needed to hear.

CHAPTER 5

Gambling On Your Future

#MoneyChat

"At the age of 61, I lost my job, home, life savings, my retirement, and my freedom. The worst thing was for my grandkids to watch me being handcuffed and put into a police car."
—Marilyn

A GAMBLING ADDICTION DOES NOT favor any one demographic. It affects all races, ages, and income levels, and many have lost their life savings, families, and careers because of it. Already a $120 billion-dollar industry in the United States, gambling is increasing with the onslaught of Internet gaming sites, new casinos, and everything in between. Often thought of as a recreational pastime, gambling becomes more than just fun for many who find themselves unable to control the urge to do it.

According to the National Council on Problem Gambling, an average of four to six million Americans are problem gamblers. Now I'm not talking about professional poker players who have honed their craft and compete against other players rather than the casino, which always wins. I'm referring to amateur poker players and casino gamblers who have become obsessed with winning and are spending their household incomes in an attempt to hit the jackpot.

Compulsive gambling is an addiction that can afflict anyone. Often, people who have overcome another addiction—smoking, drugs, alcohol—turn that same compulsive behavior toward something else, like gambling. It can turn into a vicious cycle if the behavior is not checked and an opportunity to play a game of chance—in any form—can easily get out of hand. The frequency of the habit can quickly accelerate and lead to maxed out credit cards, defaulted loans, and pawned valuables, all in an effort to get more money to gamble with. This explains why many compulsive gamblers end up filing bankruptcy. And that's just the financial damage a gambling addiction can cause. Compulsive gambling can lead to loss of employment and ruin family relationships, too.

Let's look at Marilyn L., who was never a gambler and who was 53 before she ever walked into a casino. She was hanging out with a friend at a weekend bowling tournament, and they decided to try their luck. Marilyn sat down at a slot machine and won every time she played. She couldn't believe it! She decided that this was the way to go, that she wasn't going to have to work much longer because gambling was going to make her rich!

Marilyn and her boyfriend began making the four-hour trip from her home in Yuma, Arizona, to a casino in Laughlin, Nevada every weekend but, of course, her winning streak didn't last. Soon she needed more money than her paycheck could provide. Marilyn worked as an office administrator and, though she didn't handle cash, she had access to checks. She began making checks out to herself to cover her gambling habit.

Seven years and $300,000 later, Marilyn was finally caught and sent to prison at the age of 61. The police handcuffed her at home in front of her family and grandchildren. She put it best: "I lost my job, home, life savings, my retirement and my freedom."

Then there's Bernard, who admits to using gambling as a way to escape life's issues. His choice? Lottery ticket scratch-offs. Seems harmless right? Not if you're buying them several nights a week, spending $150-$200 a pop like he was. Initially, Bernard would only buy them occasionally as a diversion, during stressful times. Eventually, he needed to escape more and more often, until he was spending most of his income gambling. Since Bernard handled the family finances, his wife didn't know that her paycheck was paying all the bills while his supported his gambling habit. She would ask where all the money was going, but Bernard would blame it on the gas the car needed for his hour and a half commute to work each day.

We also rarely talk about the weekly gambling parties, where people gather and bet on card games, sports, etc. It's harmless fun for some, but for those who are addicted due to obsessive behavior, it's eating away all their money.

I Can Afford to Gamble

It's important to recognize the difference between recreational and compulsive behavior. Recreational gamblers are able to set aside a certain amount of money, play with it and be done. But if you feel the need to keep going back, like you *must* win and will risk everything you have to do so—that's compulsive behavior and you definitely can't afford it.

Having money to gamble for fun could be part of your budget, i.e., setting aside a specific amount for recreation. But you would do that *after* your primary financial duties:

Paying bills   Investing

Saving   Giving

The balance left over after each payday is what you have fun with. Risking any of the above to gamble is a clear sign of a problem. Here's another forewarning: Is the money that you're gambling with *all* of the recreational money you have? Using all of your "fun" money to gamble is another sign that there's a problem.

Help! My Partner is Gambling Our Money Away!

You stop at the gas station to put gas in the car and your debit or credit card doesn't work. Hmm, the system must be down. So, you go inside and have the clerk swipe it for you. Sorry, ma'am/sir, but your card has been declined. Declined? You paid the bill. You know there's money in the account. But what you didn't know is that your mate has taken what's left of the money for the household expenses down to the casino. Because they just know they'll hit the jackpot this time. There are stories on top of stories about people who have depleted bank accounts without telling their mates. The money is just gone; there's no way to get it back. One woman sought help and stopped gambling for a while. She was doing fine and thought she could handle going into a casino—not for long, just for a moment.

She figured she'd spend a little money and go home. At the time she was engaged to be married. Long story short, she gambled away her savings and her fiancé's in one sitting.

FACT

According to the National Council on Problem Gambling, 20% of compulsive gamblers file bankruptcy.

If your mate is a compulsive gambler, do not live in denial. It's important that you take immediate steps to secure the household finances.

1. **Get help.** Seek counseling for your mate's gambling addiction and for your marriage/relationship. Now is not the time to be passive—unless you don't value your financial future. It is important to confront your mate seriously and let them know they will lose everything if they don't get help.

2. **Remove access.** Don't allow your mate access to the bank accounts. Review all your bank and credit card statements to make sure you are aware of all activity. Request a copy of both your credit report and your mate's to see if there is any credit card or other financial account open that you don't know about. If you have joint accounts, it's definitely time to separate them until the addiction is overcome.

3. **Take control.** You will now have to manage all the household bills and other financial responsibilities if you didn't before. Prepare yourself, as this may cause serious arguments. You will have to be strong enough to stand your ground. If you do not, your finances will continue to crumble.

DO THIS ACTION STEPS
Keys to Rebounding Financially

The key to rebounding financially in any situation is to reverse the negative behavior or situation that caused the problems. There are resources for you, so make the call, visit the websites. Do whatever it takes to break free. Counseling is key when recovering from gambling or any other addiction.

- **Counseling:** Don't try to go it alone! You need the support of an understanding community. There's no need to be embarrassed or ashamed. Put that behind you and allow yourself to be transparent enough to win this battle! Schedule a counseling session immediately. If you can't afford to pay for counseling, there are many free support groups, such as Gamblers Anonymous. At the end of this chapter is a list of U.S. and international resources you can use or share with a friend.

- **Accountability**: You need someone who will help you get on track with paying back your debts and managing your money. This may be the hardest part to handle, but until you've successfully completed your counseling sessions and are FULLY recovered, I'd suggest direct deposit for your paycheck and allowing someone you trust to manage your money, giving you cash for weekly expenses only, nothing extra.

- **Occupy your time:** Pick up a hobby, spend more time with your family—whom you've probably been neglecting due to the time you've spent gambling. Do not sit idly. Occupy your time with positive, uplifting activities so you're not tempted to gamble.

- **Stay away:** Block online casinos and gambling sites so you can't access them. In some states, you can have physical, brick-and-mortar casinos add your name to a list of people barred from entry. I definitely suggest this if it's available. Have an accountability partner who can monitor your whereabouts. Speaking of which ...

- It's time to start selling stuff and/or working extra jobs to accelerate gambling debt payback.

- Stop using credit cards and make purchases with cash only. Cut up your credit cards. Close the accounts so you aren't tempted to use them.

- Be patient. You can lose it all overnight gambling, but it will likely take you a few years to rebound. Keep notes; evaluate your progress every three months as well as each year. You'll be encouraged when you can see how far you've come, even in a short amount of time.

 SAY THIS #MONEYCHAT MANTRA

" *I (we) will no longer be bound by gambling habits*

" *I (we) will recover financially from past mistakes*

An Expert's Take
on Gambling Addiction

During this project I had the opportunity to interview Lori A. Mello, MA, LPC, MPA who is an expert in working with adults battling gambling addiction. Our interview was so insightful that I decided to publish it in its entirety below.

What is the most common thread that you see in the gambling addiction cases you come across?

It seems as if no two cases are alike and yet there are very similar stories. We see people from all walks of life—the very wealthy, very poor and the middle class. If someone is addicted and wants to gamble, he/she will find the money. Some people say to me, "Oh, I don't have a problem with gambling. I can't afford to gamble!" I tell them that people will use their whole social security or welfare check, the grocery money, the rent money, etc. to gamble. It's really not about the money per se; it's about the thrill of the chase or the escape from problems at home or at work.

Many people have lost so much by the time they call us. Their home has gone into foreclosure, they've lost their car, their job, their relationships with their family, their spouse/significant other, children—they've burned bridges with everyone. Many have stolen, embezzled and are in danger of going to jail.

A lot of folks call the help line with a similar story.

It might go something like this:

"I can't sleep. I go down to the casino (or play lottery tickets or play Bingo) every day and I feel like I can't go without it. I have no food money for the rest of the month. I'm angry with myself. The bills are piling up. I'm scared because I'm three months behind on my mortgage and my wife/husband doesn't know. They repossessed my car. I lost my job because I spent three hours gambling at lunch instead of just one, and this was the fourth or fifth time I did that."

Does recreational gambling lead to addiction or can it be something people do for fun, risk-free?

Most people who gamble recreationally do NOT turn out to be addicts. Addicts are only 2%–3% of the population. Many, many people can be recreational gamblers and be just fine. What we always ask them is, "Can you do without going [to the casino] for a month?" or "Has gambling interfered with your relationships, your work, your schooling, etc.?" or "Are you losing sleep, not eating, not paying bills, going without things because of gambling?"

What are some of the negative financial results of gambling addiction that you have seen?

Oh, wow! What a great question! The list is endless. Here are a few things:

- Loss of home

- Loss of job

- Prison time for theft/embezzlement

- Putting oneself in danger due to the unscrupulous characters they might align with to get money to pay off debts

- Getting stuck paying restitution to one's theft "victims" or to the courts for many years

- Loss of relationship with spouse, significant other, kids, etc.

- Loss of transportation

What are the steps to overcoming a gambling addiction?

1. Recognize that you have a problem.

2. Ask for help.

3. Find the root of the problem. (Why are you gambling? What are you trying to avoid? What kind of thrill does it give you?)

4. Work on recovery through replacing the gambling activity with something constructive, something that gives you hope and satisfaction.

5. Don't give up! Attend Gamblers Anonymous meetings regularly to get ongoing support.

6. Find additional support outside of your therapist. (Who in the family or among your friends might be helpful or supportive?)

How have people bounced back financially once they've overcome their addiction?

It's very tough for them. Once you are behind like that, you have to work extra hard to fully regain your wealth and your retirement savings. You can't make it up to the kids if you can't put them through college. (Some people raid their kids' college funds.) Gamblers often go on a payment plan and take debt counseling, and that helps to get their debts paid in full so they can regain some good credit and be back on the road to recovery financially. Some are so bad off, however, that they need to file for bankruptcy. Others can simply do the debt counseling and repayment plan, which is much better than bankruptcy and doesn't ruin your credit for seven years.

It's a long and painful process. Gamblers also have to learn to live on less—to spend differently, to go without. They have to learn to do everything with cash and, if they have a spouse, to allow them to pay all the bills and give them an allowance. This can be very hard, especially for men. And especially for men who have been the primary breadwinners and bill payers.

For some of your clients whose lives are filled with opportunities to gamble—at family gatherings, online, in casinos, etc. What are some alternatives that have helped them break free?

This is where "harm reduction" really comes in. Gamblers have to decide what they want to do. Many clients will tell their family, "No. I cannot participate because that is an addiction for me. Once I get started, I won't be able to quit and I'm trying to stay in recovery." They may decide to just totally abstain [from the situation], even if the gambling is part of a family function. Sometimes, however, they do what we call harm reduction, where they limit their gambling money and/or the time that they gamble. They'll say, *I'll play for one hour and spend only $50.* Many people have supportive family and friends, so they can refuse and still feel okay.

If there was one message you wish you could drill into your clients to help them overcome a gambling addiction, what would it be?

That you will NEVER win against the house [in a casino]. The odds are set AGAINST you! There is no strategy to winning on any slot machine, in any card game, with Bingo, with the lottery, scratch-offs, Keno, etc. If you are doing this because you're unhappy with yourself or you don't want to face your wife/husband or your kids or your life, spend that money on therapy. Find out why you are unhappy and fill that hole in your life with something else before it's too late!

Can you recommend any national resources?

There are a few good ones, but most are state by state. The two that are the best to contact for more information are National Council on Problem Gambling (**www. ncpgambling.org**) and National Center for Responsible Gaming (**www.ncrg.org**).

RESOURCES!

National:

- Gamblers Anonymous (**www.gamblersanonymous.org**): an online international directory of meetings for those with gambling concerns and for the spouses, family and friends of gamblers

- U. S. National Gambling helpline (**www.ncpgambling.org**): 24-hour hotline, 1-800-522-4700

- Debtors Anonymous (**www.debtorsanonymous.org**) Phone: 781-453-2743, Fax: 781-453-2745

- Women Helping Women (**www.femalegamblers.info**): news and support for women in recovery

- Stop Predatory Gambling Foundation-U.S. (http://stoppredatorytorygambling.org/): resources to support the view that legalized gambling is harmful to individuals, communities and society

International*

- Canadian Gambling Hotline: 1-888-391-1111

- Australia's Gamblers Anonymous (**www.gamblersanonymous.org. au**) provides information on GA meetings throughout Australia.

- GamCare-UK (**www.gamcare.org**) is a UK-based registered charity that provides counseling and advice through their helpline, face to face and through an online forum. GamCare-UK also provides education/awareness programs for young people.

- Gamb–ling (**www.gamb-ling.com**) provides multilingual information, awareness, and prevention.

- Gamtalk (**www.gamtalk.org**) is an online support community for those with gambling issues.

- Safe Harbor Compulsive Gambling Hub (**www.sfcghub.com**) is a chat room and posting board for gamblers.

- New Zealand Problem Gambling Helpline (**www.gambling helpline.co.nz**) is a free, national phone support service that also offers referrals, information, and website support.

- Problem Gambling Foundation of New Zealand (**www.pgfnz.org. nz**) offers free counseling across New Zealand for problem gamblers, their families and others affected by problem gambling

*Source: **www.problemgambling.ca***

GamBlock—Software that blocks access to Internet gambling sites. It helps people with gambling problems avoid the dangers of online gambling. Prices range from $35.00 to $70.00; **www.gamblock.com**.

NOTE: Parents, I'd definitely suggest installing this software on your teen's computers. There's an alarming number of teenagers gambling online without their parents' knowledge. Also, check their iPads and cell phones for games of chance. Below are more resources—grab a downloadable list at dorethiakelly.com/moneychathub

SECTION TWO

Getting on Solid Ground

CHAPTER 6

Get Your Money Right!

#MoneyChat

"You don't have to be a miser, just be wiser with your money."
—Dorethia Kelly

IN ORDER TO MAKE YOUR money grow, you have to manage it properly. It's important to get beyond having just enough or barely making it so you can focus on the larger financial picture—creating a nest egg for the next generation in your family.

STEP 1: Make a Decision

Making a decision to better manage your money is the first step to getting on solid financial ground. When you get tired of riding the same merry-go–round—never having enough money, hiding from creditors, facing financial emergencies—it will definitely be decision time! Now, this doesn't mean you'll get it right every time, but you will keep going in the right direction, learning along the way and never giving up. Eventually, you'll find that you make fewer financial mistakes and there's money in the bank!

It's not that easy? Okay, here's a little exercise. Get a sticky note and write down everything you'd be able to do if you only had to pay for necessities— that is, if you didn't have to make any debt payments.

Now write down how that makes you feel. Relieved? Like a burden is lifted? Happy? Stick that note up in various places throughout your home to remind you of your aim. Use it to light a fire in you toward making the decision to take action!

STEP 2: GET BUSY! Be Your Own Financial Coach!

1. Educate yourself

What are you reading about money? Don't let social scrolling take up all your time! Set aside time each week to read at least three articles about personal finances and money management. Everything won't apply, but the more you learn, the quicker you'll be able to determine what's good advice for you. Look up terms and words you're not familiar with.

2. Set financial goals

Write out your goals. What do you want to accomplish financially? Take small steps; don't think you have to write that you'll be debt free in three months if you know that isn't feasible. And don't only write down the goal, write how you will achieve it.

Example:

This Year ...

1. *I want to completely pay off one bill in six months by paying an extra $25 per month.*

2. *I want to save $50 per pay period, each month, by buying lunch only on Fridays.*

Three-year Financial Goals...Five-year Financial Goals ...10-year Financial Goals ...

3. Know your numbers!

Remember, managing money is really just simple math. What you have coming in vs. what's going out. As I said before, all you need is pen and paper and a list of your bills with their due dates.

Create four lists:

- **Income**—Amount of money you have coming in from all sources.

- **Expenses/Bills**—What bills and household expenses do you pay each month, quarter, etc.?

- **Current assets**—Any investments, savings or other valuables you may have, like that money in the safe under the floorboards (wink, wink).

- **Current debt**—For debts that you may or may not be paying monthly, what is the total balance due and monthly payment amount? If you were able to pay it off today, how much would it take to do so?

3. Develop a system

Do not freak out! This simply means having a schedule for paying bills/ budgeting, paying off debt, saving/investing and reviewing your progress.

Here's an easy system to follow:

Budget:

- Budget bi-weekly or monthly.

- Choose a "light," less busy day where you'll be able to focus quietly for an hour. For me, it's early Saturday morning before the house (my family) wakes up.

When writing out your budget, don't just consider the current month. Do three months at a time, at a minimum. This allows you to plan for the future months and re-adjust as needed.

You can access your free budget templates at dorethiakelly.com/moneychathub

SAMPLE MONTHLY BUDGET
Family of four, monthly net income of $4,200

	JANUARY		FEBRUARY		MARCH	
	Budget	Actual	Budget	Actual	Budget	Actual
INCOME	$4,200.00	$4,200.00	$4,200.00		$4,200.00	
EXPENSES:						
Tithes/Giving	-300.00	-300.00	-300.00		-300.00	
Savings:	-300.00	-300.00	-300.00		-300.00	
Housing						
Rent/Mortgage	-750.00	-750.00	-750.00		-750.00	
Renters/Home Ins.	-100.00	-100.00	-100.00		-100.00	
Utilities						
Electric	-50.00	-44.00	-50.00		-50.00	
Gas	-100.00	-125.00	-100.00		-100.00	
Water	-35.00	-35.00	-35.00		-35.00	
Transportation						
Car Pmt	-325.00	-325.00	-325.00		325.00	
Car Ins.	-175.00	-175.00	-175.00		-175.00	
Gas	-400.00	-375.00	-400.00		-400.00	
Repairs						
Food						
Groceries	-450.00	-525.00	-450.00		-450.00	
Eating Out	-100.00	-75.00	-100.00		-100.00	
Household						
Toiletries	-100.00	-55.00	-100.00		-100.00	
Cleaning, etc.	-20.00		-20.00		-20.00	

	JANUARY		FEBRUARY		MARCH	
	Budget	Actual	Budget	Actual	Budget	Actual
INCOME	$4,200.00	$4,200.00	$4,200.00		$4,200.00	
EXPENSES:						
Clothing						
Kids	-100.00	-125.00	-100.00		-100.00	
Adults	-175.00	0.00	-175.00		-175.00	
Grooming						
Kids	-20.00	0.00	-20.00		-20.00	
Adults	-100.00	-100.00	-100.00		-100.00	
School Expenses						
Kids	-50.00		-50.00		-50.00	
Adults	-300.00		-300.00		-300.00	
Entertainment/Gifts						
Parties/Birthdays		-35.00				
Movies/Concerts		-120.00				
Holidays						
TOTAL EXPENSES	$-3950.00	$-3564.00	$-3950.00	$-3950.00		
BALANCE (Income—Expenses)	$250.00	$636.00	$250.00	$250.00		

In this example, the month of January is over and the budgeted and actual spending amounts have been entered. February and March are projected spending amounts. As each item is paid during the month, you write in the actual amount spent.

Budgeted vs. Actual:

In the example above the difference between budgeted and actual for January: $386

If you see that you're going over or under budget regularly, you need to adjust your spending. For example, if you budget $350 for groceries each month, but consistently spend $450, that is probably the amount you should budget for. If it's a stretch, see where else you can cut to fund it. If you find that you budget $250 each month for clothes, but only spend $175, lower your budgeted amount for clothes.

Eliminating Debt

Based on the numbers in your budget, is there anything left to add toward getting rid of debt faster? If yes, begin using most (if not all) of that surplus to pay off the smallest debt first.

Investing

If you are currently investing, determine whether you can contribute more each month. If you are tackling debt now, decide on a date—whether it's next year or in the next three years—that you'll be able to start investing.

I encourage investing after you've paid off as much debt as possible and only have larger amounts to bite off. Until then, all extra money should go toward getting rid of those smaller debts.

Quarterly Review

It's important to track how you're doing. Over the years, I noticed that it worked better for my clients to have a timeline for review that would serve as a reminder, so I suggest a quarterly schedule. As the seasons change, you know it's time for a checkup!

During your review, ask yourself honest questions. The point is to be making headway toward your goals. Are you consistently budgeting and sticking to it? If not, what needs to be adjusted? How much debt have you been able to pay off? Did you open that mutual fund account? Get that second job? If you had a setback or you aren't where you wanted to be, don't beat yourself up about it, just start over!

3. Accountability

Who do you know that is good with money? If you're married, think of a couple that's good with money. Who can you trust to discuss major financial decisions with?

I have a great group of friends. They reel me in when I'm in the deep end and encourage me when I need it. We need people like that when it comes to our finances. You should have one or two people in your circle that you can learn from when it comes to finances.

I know money is a personal and touchy subject—we don't want others to know how much we do or don't have, or how much we may not know about money. I understand and I'm not suggesting that you run to everyone you know and tell them your business. But think of a couple of people who are smart with their money. You can tell by their conversation and actions. I'm not talking about people who brag about what they have or look like they have it all together. No, find people who talk about things like saving and investing more than spending, people who talk about retirement accounts, getting out of debt and preparing their kids for college, and who are practicing what they preach.

A word about budgeting: I know there are a million schools of thought on this subject. Some say it's useless because people hate to do it and never will. Some try to do it mentally and end up miscalculating, forgetting about money spent, etc. I'm sorry but writing out your budget is the first basic action you must take in successfully handling your money. It allows you to see how much money you will or won't have over several weeks/months so you can plan. It helps eliminate financial surprises from popping up.

I don't yell "YIPPEE!" every time I sit down to do my budget, but it's a necessary practice so I know where my money is going. And budgeting now is super easy with all the apps that are available and online banking. Once you put your info in once, you can simply adjust as needed.

I suggest you budget and pay bills bi-weekly or monthly. This allows you to better manage your time and it's not as much of a chore. Having to do it every week may be too much for some and cause them to stop altogether. So, whether it's pen and paper, a spreadsheet or an app on your phone, get 'er done!

 ## DO THIS ACTION STEPS

Create your budget/spending plan using the templates found here **dorethiakelly.com/moneychathub**

 ## SAY THIS #MONEYCHAT MANTRA

" *I am smart with my money*

" *I am worthy of financial success*

" *I live financially free*

" *I budget every month*

Lamont: Living the Single Life and Paying Myself First

As a single man with children, dating can be a challenge if not carefully planned out. Disposable income is hard to come by sometimes. While managing my bills (rent, utilities, etc.), I also want to have fun with the leftover funds from working so hard.

When discussing this with Dorethia, she emphasized a very important point that I took to heart. "One who saves early can afford big things for a longer time frame." Her suggestion was to "pay myself first," being prudent with my net income minus any bills I've already paid. The key is to set a target for savings just as if I owed myself a large bill that I had to pay in installments. Once I deducted that amount, she suggested a "dating fund" for me. We laughed about it, the thought was hilarious to me, but I started doing it anyway. It worked, I set aside a certain amount I wanted to spend each pay on my single life activities. When the funds had been exhausted, that was it. No more dates or nights out with the guys. It worked and I was fine with it because I was able to get out and have fun while saving money for my future.

This saving mindset also helped with the purchase of my current vehicle. I had been looking to upgrade, but with my previous car paid off, I wasn't interested in financing a car note. Unfortunately, insurance can be expensive where I live as I reside in an urban area. As a matter of fact, insurance is so expensive that many times the cost exceeds what you would have paid for your monthly car premium.

Attempting to avoid this, I followed the same theme of paying myself first. The first step was deciding on how much I wanted to spend. I finally conceded to selecting a used car as the insurance typically wouldn't be as much. Because I live in a no-fault state, I could elect to lower my cost even more. I scoured many online sites and figured that a late model vehicle between $4,000 and $5,000 would suit me just fine. Knowing the time frame in which I wanted to purchase the car, I divided my biweekly pays into a reasonable amount and deposited into an account that was hard to access (to keep me honest). I did this by opening up an account with no debit card so if I needed funds, I would have to physically go to the credit union. To deposit money, I could just mail in a money order.

As I got into the habit of contributing to my "car bank," the process felt extremely fulfilling. Eventually, I hit my goal, selected a vehicle, had it inspected, and voila! I had the car I really wanted at an economical price. Plus, calculating that an average car note for a new car would have been at least $350 (once again, not including the *high* insurance in my area), paying for the car in full, in this case $4,200, meant that I essentially paid myself back in about twelve months, if not less.

In summary, I found that when I applied Dorethia's words of wisdom to pay myself first, the rewards I reaped were transferable across many goals. I really appreciate the advice she gave me.

The Durden Family

We are a blended family. My husband and I started dating around the time we found out how much money he was to pay in child support, which was and still is a lot. We dated for two years before getting married. I have two daughters, ages seven and four, and he has a daughter and a son, ages eight and three.

I have always loved learning about money and budgeting; it's fun to me. My husband's relationship with money was a different story. But, when we realized that we had to differentiate between what we needed and what we wanted, his eyes opened as well. I began following every money management website and expert on Facebook and Twitter, which is how I found Dorethia's #MoneyChat. I loved the guests and advice from participants; it showed me I was not alone on my path. My goal was to discover different perspectives on money management and what we could apply to our finances.

With all the information I was learning, we began to make life changes. My husband got rid of his new vehicle and got a fifteen-year-old car. My truck is twelve years old. We decided to live off one paycheck, so we researched a low-cost area to live. Of course, as soon as you begin to get on a positive path, challenges come. In the first two years we were together, not only did we spend 40 percent of his check to support his children, but I also lost my job. Good thing we were living on one paycheck and saving money. Because we eliminated cable, car loans, eating out, and always looked for bargains, we were still able to eliminate all our debt in the same time frame. We paid off approximately

$45,000 in debt ($25,000 was eliminated when he sold his truck). We were also able to take the *entire summer off* to spend with our children.

My husband and I were both in the military, which afforded us the opportunity to attend college without student loans; we both earned our bachelor's degrees. My husband was still on active duty, so the Army paid his tuition. Since I am a veteran, I used my GI Bill to pay for about 75 percent of my education costs. We paid the other 25 percent out of pocket.

When my husband was preparing to leave the military, he was required to take a budgeting class, which was a real eye opener for him. He always trusted that I knew why we were being frugal, but the class made him realize just how important it was. We complement each other in that he helps me see that sometimes we need to spend a little to create family memories and I make sure we don't spend too much.

We decided that our children need memories and experiences, not presents. We have fun every day and, most of the time, for free. We have picnics, go to playgrounds and on hikes, and share memories by making things from scratch. Now that we are debt free and have some money in savings for emergencies and other things, we are definitely feeling more relaxed and enjoying life more.

CHAPTER 7

The Infamous Emergency Fund

#MoneyChat

"An emergency fund allows you to be prepared for the unexpected stress free."
—Dorethia Kelly

"THAT WILL BE $2,500, MA'AM."

"Whoa! What?"

"Yes. There's a lot of body damage. You'll need two new doors, front end work and paint."

My heart began to pound and suddenly my stomach didn't feel so good. I walked back to my beat-up truck, climbed in and cried that big, ugly, mouth wide open cry. As I was driving home from work that week, a kid slammed into my driver's side while pulling out of a gas station. I had worked hard to pay off my truck early and then, being even more ambitious, I dropped my insurance coverage down to a basic policy—which meant this repair wasn't covered. (I'll never do that again!) I had no money in the bank and had never had $2,500 at any given time anyway. I had no idea how I was going to pay for the repair. I was already overextended and couldn't add anymore bills, and I refused to borrow any money.

I had been caught like this many, many times. Financial emergencies would come up and I'd have no way of covering them. As a single mother with two kids, there was never really any "extra money." One day, I was browsing through a website and saw an article about an emergency fund. *Now what is that?* I thought. As I began to read the article, I knew this was going to be the first step toward changing my financial future.

Emergency Fund: [ih-mur-juhn-see fuhnd]

A supply of money set aside for unexpected financial issues.

Game Changer:

From then on, I began to read as much as I could about handling my money differently, saving money and, yes, building an emergency fund. It worked! I was elated! But even more than that, I was relieved. It took some time, but I was able to actually save by changing my habits one by one.

Down the road, other financial emergencies arose—the refrigerator had to be replaced, there were more car repairs, unexpected medical bills, etc. But I was prepared. There was no need for tears or that feeling of dread and despair because I could write a check! Wooo Hooo! Not only that, but my conversation changed. Instead of complaining about my money, I was telling my family and friends how they could avoid being broke all the time and succeed with their money. You can, too! Keep reading!

How Much Should You Save?

An emergency fund allows you to breathe easier when financial issues come up and, trust me, they will come up! How much you save depends on your comfort level, but the minimum, initially, should be $1,000. Young adults or those with extremely tight budgets may want to ease into it and start with $250, then $500, and finally build up to $1,000. And then savers and couples who can afford it may be able to save $2,500, initially.

There are two phases of saving for emergencies:

PHASE 1

Saving for things that come up throughout the year. Once you've reached your goal, you can stop adding to the fund and re-allocate the money you were putting toward it to paying down debt. Be sure to maintain $1,000 in the fund at all times.

PHASE 2

Saving nine to 12 months of expenses (not income) to cover major situations, such as a job loss or a medical emergency, *after* you've paid off all or majority of your debt. The debt I'm talking about here does *not* include your mortgage. That can be taken care of later, once your financial footing is more stable.

Now don't let saving nine to 12 months of expenses scare you. You'll still be able to live. Remember—you'll be working from your budget and all spending will be accounted for, even the fun spending! Set milestones. Save one month of expenses, three months, six months and so on until you reach your 12-month goal. Also remember—by now you will have paid down some debt, so you'll be able to save more money.

How to Save FOR Your Emergency Fund

It's time to get creative, especially if your budget is stretched to its limits. If you're already in the red each month, you'll definitely have to focus on increasing your income to cover your normal household bills. Slow and steady wins the race. Pay the monthly amounts on your normal household bills, and any additional money brought in goes toward your emergency fund.

Think about every area you may be able to save. For instance, if your cable bill is $100 per month, you could save $1,000 if you went without cable for 10 months. After you've reached your goal, you can have your cable back. That may even be an incentive to save faster!

MORE MONTH THAN MONEY? PAY THESE FIRST!

HOUSING—Pay your rent or mortgage first. You need a place to lay your head and you want to provide stability for your family

UTILITIES—Yeah, let's keep the lights and heat on. This is part of that stability mentioned above.

GROCERIES—When it comes time to cut, most people skimp on groceries. They buy junk with no nutritional value because it's cheaper.

Well, I certainly hope you aren't at Whole Foods if you need to cut back, but it's important to feed your family healthy meals. Go to farmers markets and catch sales in order to save money.

TRANSPORTATION—If you can't get to work, you won't have a job long, so make sure you have transportation, whatever form it may be in. Again, this doesn't mean you should run out and lease that new luxury ride! Be sensible, just be sure you can get back and forth to work.

LADIES

Hair and nails can really add up. I know—this is sacred ground and I truly understand. But add up how much you're spending on yourself and your daughters each month. A few months of sacrifice would get you closer to your goal.

FELLAS

Men's grooming has gone up in recent years as well. It's time well spent to learn how to cut your own hair… or make sure you add the expense in your spending plan.

SINGLE FELLAS

The dating scene and hanging out with the guys can really put a cramp in your wallet and saving goals. I have a friend who said that, thanks to me, he's started a dating fund. That's right, an amount he can spend each month taking a young lady out to dinner, to a movie, etc. Or even just ordering in for movie nights. Food delivery adds up! When the fund is empty—no more dating for the month.

I've got an idea! What if everyone focused on their emergency fund for a few months and seriously cut your "hanging out" money? It's not forever, just until you reach your goal. Sounds like a plan to me! Whaddya think??

DIG DEEP

Sometimes we can find money in places we never thought of looking. For instance, do you have investments, bonds, etc. that you can liquidate? Do you have valuables you can sell? Sites like eBay, Amazon and other social selling sites have made it easier than ever to sell things we aren't using anymore. Take inventory of your home, garage, basement etc. to see what you can get rid of to bring in extra money.

Okay, Dorethia. I've got nothing. There's no extra money anywhere! Well then, it's time to increase your income. It's time to look for another job in addition to your main gig and let go of all pride. That's right—it doesn't matter what the job is, as long as it pays. I've coached clients who earn well into the six figures, yet have no savings and live paycheck to paycheck. I tell them the same thing. Find a part-time job—or two!

Think of five things you can do for extra money, with the least amount of cash outlay. If you need ideas, check out the list at the end of this chapter. Here are a few to start with:

- **Home Cleaning**—All you need is a mop, a bucket, some cleaning supplies and you're in business pretty quickly!

- **Handyman**—Painting, garage cleaning, minor home repairs— these are especially helpful to seniors and single parents.

- **Auto Repair**—Brakes, oil changes, tune-ups—small jobs you can do from home.

- **eBay/Amazon**—It's easy to sell items online. I have a friend who finds cheap books at library sales, yard sales, etc. and re-sells them online.

- **Take a Class**—Community colleges often offer cheap classes in areas that you could turn into a profitable side business, e.g., landscaping, crafts, hair braiding, graphic design, minor auto repair, etc.

At the end of this chapter, I share more ways to make extra money!

Where to Stash Your Savings

Your emergency fund is not to be considered an investment, so you wouldn't save it in a mutual fund, buy stock with it or otherwise invest it. This is cash that you need to be able to access right away if necessary. Therefore, it should be kept in a high-yield savings account, which has a higher interest rate than a traditional savings account. In the beginning, when you are building up to your

$1,000, you may have to begin with a traditional savings account, then switch to a high-yield account once your balance has reached the minimum required. While the money is sitting and waiting for the inevitable financial situation or emergency to come up, it may as well collect as much interest as possible.

That's NOT an Emergency

Okay, let's get a few things straight. An emergency fund is not simply extra money. It has a goal, which is to keep you financially stable when the storms are raging. This means there's no room for any "I deserve it" or "pity party" purchases. This is about reaching your financial goals. If you use the money in your emergency fund to go shopping every time you're upset, feeling low or get distracted by some new car, tool or tech item that depreciates in value, you will be out of luck when an actual emergency occurs. So, hands off! You want it to be there when you need it.

You know what else is NOT an emergency? Family members who are low on cash. If you have a tendency to go into your pocket when family comes calling, set up a separate fund for that. Seriously.

So, what does qualify as an emergency? Medical bills, car repairs, unexpected or necessary expenses for the kids, unexpected bills, a job loss, etc. The key word is *unexpected*—things that aren't part of your normal monthly expenses, but that you definitely must pay.

As for new furniture, household items, etc.—these are purchases you plan for. As long as you have something to sit on, you don't *need* new furniture. But if you *want* new furniture, save for it and buy it with cash.

What Happens When You Dip Into It?

Don't feel bad when you have to dip into your emergency fund. That's what it's there for. Many people are discouraged when they actually have to cover a financial emergency. While we all wish we could avoid them, they're a part of life! Instead, be thankful that you have some money saved and work toward replenishing the account.

It's key to be disciplined about putting the money back. This means you do the same thing you did to fund it in the first place, i.e., work extra jobs find something to sell and put all extra money into the account until you're back at your goal.

More Money-Making Ideas!

✔ Babysitting

✔ Senior citizen care: cooking, cleaning, transporting, etc.

✔ Tutor students in-person or online in a subject you excel in, e.g., math, science, essay writing, etc.

✔ Landscaping and lawn care

✔ Pet-sit for neighbors on vacation or walk dogs.

✔ Become a virtual assistant for business owners. Check out **www. fiverr.com** or **www.upwork.com**.

✔ Detail cars.

✔ Good with computers? Teach seniors the basics.

✔ Transcription service

✔ Plant a garden and sell your produce. Better yet, teach others how to create their own garden!

✔ Sell baked goods to neighbors or at a local farmers market and during holidays.

✔ Write an e-book and sell it online.

✔ Garage clean up service

✔ Website design, graphic design, flyers, posters

✔ Are you artistic? Create paintings/drawings/poetry and sell them.

✔ Are you musically inclined? Not only can you sing or play an instrument at weddings and other events, you can also teach students/adults who want to learn.

Legit Remote Work Opportunities!

If you aren't entrepreneurial and want to work a side-gig, no worries—I've got you too! here's a list of legit companies that you can work for from home.

- Transcribeme.com

- MicroWorkers.com

- Truelancers.com

- RatRaceRebellion.com

- LiveOps.com

- WorkingSolutions.com

- ZoomAudits.com.

- CGEVirtualSolutions.com

- Pearson.Jobs.com

- Careers.Concentrix.com

- WorkForWhat.com

Grab both of these lists at **dorethiakelly.com/moneychathub**

 DO THIS ACTION STEPS: Your List of Five!

1. List five spending habits you can cut in order to save for your emergency fund.

2. List five things you can do to earn extra money.

3. Go through each room of your home and look for at least five things you can sell. Don't forget the garage and basement.

4. Every day for five days, work on a strategy for adding money to your emergency fund. At the end of a work week, you should have a plan!

 ## SAY THIS #MONEYCHAT MANTRAS

" *An emergency fund will provide me financial safety*

" *I am serious about saving for emergencies*

Congratulations! You are on your way! I'd love to hear about your progress! Shoot me a message any time at hey@dorethiakelly.com!

The Cordaways: Emergency Fund Hijacked by the Unexpected

With a family of four, my husband and I each kept an eye on the finances. What we needed was a system, a written plan, and more of a financial cushion. We would start our emergency fund but weren't able to increase it because of unexpected expenses. We reached out to Dorethia to help us tighten up our budgeting, especially for inconsistent miscellaneous expenses.

It seemed that our money on miscellaneous items was going into a black hole. We were good with shopping for groceries and clothes and paying the mortgage since they were a set amount each month. It was the small things that came up that caused problems and threw our budget out of whack. We would try to pay for them quickly without looking into other deals or calling around. This behavior prevented us from saving as much as we wanted to.

For instance, when the need for a new musical instrument came up, we decided to rent. Done, right?

Well, not exactly. Dorethia showed us how buying a used one at a reasonable price was much smarter financially. On another occasion, my kids needed routine physicals and lab work. In order to get both services done by our doctor, I ended up paying for the lab work, which would have been free had I gone to another location to have it done. That was a needless expense in the name of convenience.

Working with Dorethia was very eye opening. As she helped us match our behaviors and spending habits with the numbers, we realized what was stopping us from reaching our goals. We developed a fund for unexpected, irregular expenses and added a line item in our budget to account for them and our emergency fund. We are now better able to forecast those expenses throughout the year and know how much extra we can put toward savings each month.

If the money isn't there, we wait. Even if we have it, we often still wait to ensure we aren't spending unnecessarily and not getting the biggest bang for our buck.

CHAPTER 8

How To Fix
Your Credit Yourself

#MoneyChat

"It's not the load that breaks you down, it's the way you carry it."
—Lena Horne

GOOD CREDIT IS A KEY that can unlock the door to better insurance quotes and better interest rates on credit cards and loans. Poor credit, on the other hand, is expensive and *inconvenient*.

Creditors typically charge you more to borrow money when your credit is less-than-stellar. Poor credit also means you may have to pay a higher security deposit when you rent or your rental applications could get denied altogether. The good news is, you can build or rebuild credit if you have no credit history or poor credit history.

What Credit Is and How It Works

Your "credit" is a term used to explain how good or bad you are at paying the money back that you borrow. Credit reports and credit scores are what lenders, landlords, and others use to determine how creditworthy you are.

What's on your credit report?

Your credit report lists information like your accounts (including credit cards, student loans, retail accounts, etc.), payment history, and public records. The information comes from data reported by creditors to the three credit bureaus—Experian, Equifax, and TransUnion.

When you make payments, your account issuer reports those payments to the credit bureaus. If you miss payments, the account issuer reports those missed payments as well. Missed payments are a sign to future creditors that you may have trouble paying bills. To protect themselves from financial risk, they could deny you credit or charge you a higher interest rate.

What's your credit score?

Your credit score is a three-digit grade of what's on your credit report. There are different scoring models, but the FICO credit score is the one most commonly used.[9] FICO credit scores range from 300 to 850, with 850 being the best possible score. Here are the score ranges:

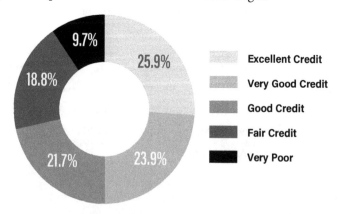

- 9.7%
- 25.9%
- 18.8%
- 21.7%
- 23.9%

- Excellent Credit
- Very Good Credit
- Good Credit
- Fair Credit
- Very Poor

Credit score requirements can vary from lender to lender, but you typically need to be in the "good" range or better to qualify for the best interest rates on mortgages, auto loans, and personal loans.

Another credit scoring model is the Vantage Score. It started with a different credit scoring range than FICO initially, but eventually adopted the 530–850 model as well and is now used widely by lenders to determine creditworthiness.

How Your Credit Score Is Calculated

There are five factors from your credit report that impact your FICO credit score.[10] Here are the factors in detail and organized by level of importance:

- **Payment history (35% of your score)**—Your history of paying on your accounts.

- **Amounts owed (30% of your score)**—Your total debt and this factor includes a comparison of your credit card debt balances to your credit limits.

- **Length of credit history (15% of your score)**—How long you've been managing credit.

- **Credit mix (10% of your score)**—The type of credit you have, such as installment loans, revolving credit, and retail accounts. A mix of different accounts can be positive for your score.

- **New credit (10% of your score)**—How many new accounts and credit inquiries you have. Hard inquiries caused by credit applications can impact your score negatively; meanwhile, soft inquiries (done by an employer's background check or by you checking your own credit) do not impact your score.

As you can see, payment history has the most influence on your credit score, so you want to make sure that you're always making at least minimum payments on your debt accounts. An adverse history that arises from high debt balances and long-term missed payments—such as repossession, accounts in collections, or bankruptcy—will have the worst impact on your score.

Fortunately, having adverse history doesn't mean you're doomed forever. Rebuilding can take time, but it can be done! Late payments generally stay on your report for up to seven years and bankruptcy for up to 10 years.[11] As time passes, your positive current history starts outweighing the past negative history. Eventually, the negative hits against your report will be erased.

Credit Utilization—Don't Skip This

The next important factor is "amounts owed" which considers how much debt you have in total.[12] Your credit utilization ratio is considered under this factor and is an important component to monitor. Credit utilization compares your total credit card balances to your total credit limits. You should keep your utilization below 30% which means you should use no more than 30% of your available credit. To calculate your credit utilization, follow these steps:

1. Write down all of your credit card balances and add them up.

2. Write down all of your credit card limits and add them up.

3. Divide your balance total (Step 1) by your credit limit total (Step 2).

4. Multiply the result by 100 to get a percentage.

Here's an example:

$3,300/$12,500 = .264

.264 x 100 = 26.4%

CREDIT CARD	BALANCE	CREDIT LIMIT
Credit Card 1	$500	$2,000
Credit Card 2	$2,000	$2,500
Credit Card 3	$200	$3,000
Credit Card 4	$600	$5,000
TOTAL CREDIT UTILIZATION = 26.4%	$3,300	$12,500

Your credit utilization is a factor that can make or break your score, and it's something that you can work on today. Paying off some of your credit card debt may have a faster impact on your score than establishing a better payment history since that takes some time. Use tips from Chapter 1 to crush your balances. If you pay off credit cards, consider keeping them open. The available credit you're not using on active accounts can have a positive impact on your score.

How to Pull Your Free Credit Report

Now that we've covered the basics, it's time to see where you stand by pulling your credit report. Every 12 months, you can get a free credit report from each of the three national credit bureaus at AnnualCreditReport.com.

This credit report doesn't come with a credit score—we'll talk about how to get that next. If you've already gotten your free yearly reports, you may be able to get a free report from credit report websites like Credit Karma or Credit Sesame. Remember, pulling your credit score is a soft inquiry that doesn't affect your score.

How to Get Your FICO Score

To get your FICO score, first check with your bank, credit union, or credit card company. Some financial institutions like banks and credit unions offer free FICO scores. If you don't get one there for free, you could buy score monitoring from myFICO.com. It costs about $19 to $39 per month, depending on the plan.

You've probably noticed there are free sites that market free credit scores as well. Often, these sites offer free VantageScores instead of an actual FICO score. Although it's not a FICO score, similar factors—such as your payment history and debt balances—go into calculating your VantageScore. So, if you choose to monitor your VantageScore for free and you see some improvement, there's a chance that your FICO score is improving as well.

5 Ways to Build Credit

Building credit may not happen overnight, but there are small consistent steps you can take to get your score moving in the right direction.

1. Dispute Errors or Incomplete Records

According to the Fair Credit Reporting Act, credit bureaus must only report accurate, complete, and current records.[13] Negative records are generally supposed to fall off after seven to 10 years. If you dispute an incorrect or old record that can't be verified, it must be removed.

Mail disputes through certified mail to each credit bureau that's reporting incorrect information. I know, we rarely use mail these days, but this seems to still be an effective way to communicate with reporting agencies. Add a copy of the report with the problems circled and include your explanation of why it should be removed in the letter. You should also send a dispute letter to the account issuer that's reporting the incorrect information. Here's where to send your disputes:

EXPERIAN	www.experian.com/disputes	P.O. Box 4500, Allen, TX 75013	Experian.com
EQUIFAX	www.equifax.com/personal/credit-report-services/credit-dispute/	P.O. Box 740256, Atlanta, GA 30374	Equifax.com
TRANSUNION	www.transunion.com/credit-disputes/dispute-your-credit	Consumer Dispute Center P.O. Box 2000, Chester, PA 19016	Transunion.com

2. Make at Least Minimum Payments

Since payment history is the most influential credit factor, your top priority should be making on-time payments from this day forward. If you do slip up, don't *give up*! The longer the payment is late, the more of an impact it has on your score. A payment that's 30 days late may not impact you as much as a 60- or 90-day late payment, so pay off the balance as soon as you can.[14]

3. Reduce Your Balances

4. Use a Secured Card or Consider a Credit Builder Loan

If you are new to credit or you have a bankruptcy, repossession, or collections account on your record, you may have trouble qualifying for unsecured credit to build or rebuild positive history. In this scenario, you can consider a secured card or credit builder loan. Here's how both work:

- A secured card is one where you have to put down a deposit first. Payments on the card are reported to the bureaus to help you build credit. Once you prove that you can keep up with payments, the creditor may offer you a regular card that doesn't require a deposit.

- A credit builder loan is like a secured card in a loan format. You apply for a loan and the lump sum is put into a separate account that you can't touch. You make loan payments, and payments are reported to the bureaus. Once the loan is paid off, you get the lump sum. Some credit unions[15][16] offer credit builders loans, so check there first. If not, you can consider a company like Self that specializes in credit builder loans.

5. Avoid Many Hard Inquiries

Having many hard inquiries on your account can be a sign to lenders that you're a credit risk. Only apply for new credit with intention and when you can manage payments. The one caveat to this is if you're shopping for a loan for a home or car. In this case, applying for multiple loans to compare offers within 30 days is considered rate shopping and may count as one hard inquiry. This has less of an impact than applying for multiple credit cards one after the other.

When Does Your Credit Report Update?

If you take steps to build credit, you may be wondering when you'll see a score improvement. Typically, lenders report records to credit bureaus once per month. But this can happen at the beginning of the month, mid-month, or the end of the month. If you sign up for regular credit report monitoring, your most current payment may or may not show up on your latest monthly report depending on when you pay.

For example, if you pay a credit card bill on the first day of the month and the company reports payments on the 30th of each month, you may not see that payment on your report until the next month. If you pay on the 29th, it would appear on your report within a few days because you paid before the report date.

Tip—Rapid Rescoring: You can call your lender's credit department and ask which day of the month they report to the credit bureaus so you can plan accordingly. There's also something called "rapid rescoring." If you're buying a house and you pay off debt, your lender may be able to request a rescore. A rescore that produces a better credit score could qualify you for a better home loan.

What You Need to Know About Credit Repair

We read about credit and debt counseling agencies in the debt chapter, so please re-visit that section. I want to reiterate that there are both reputable credit repair companies and non-reputable credit repair companies. It's illegal for a credit repair company to promise results or charge you upfront fees, so watch out for scams.[17] If you decide to work with a credit repair company be sure to read reviews, and understand all fees involved.

Credit repair is something you can do on your own if you're persistent. Your score may not skyrocket overnight, but you should see incremental improvements as you consistently make on-time payments and work toward reducing your debt balances.

I'd love for you to share your credit building progress with me! Follow me on **Instagram and Twitter as @dorethiakelly**. You can always shoot me an email at **hey@dorethiakelly.com** as well!

 DO THIS **ACTION STEPS**

1. **Visit dorethiakelly.com/moneychathub** for credit dispute templates

2. **Pull your credit report and scores:** If you haven't done this after reading the debt chapter, here's your reminder… mmm… hmmm. Get your free credit reports from AnnualCreditReport. com or from another free credit reporting site to review the records on each of your accounts. See if your financial institution offers free credit scores. If not, you can get your FICO score from

myFICO.com or you can get free VantageScores from Credit Karma or Credit Sesame.

3. **Audit your report for errors:** Go carefully through each one of the records on your credit reports to ensure they are accurate and current. Circle negative records that don't belong to you and that are incorrect or outdated.

5. **Go online to dispute your records:** Email or use the online dispute section of each credit bureau that's reporting the incorrect or old data explaining why it should be removed.

6. **Compare secured cards and credit builder loan options:** If you're considering building credit with a secured card or credit builder loan, compare fees and the deposit required before choosing a product.

 ## SAY THIS #MONEYCHAT MANTRA

" *I have excellent credit*

" *I pay all my bills on time*

" *Creditors no longer call me for past due debts*

SECTION THREE

Growing Your Money

CHAPTER 9

Investing 101:
The Basics

#MoneyChat

"Rocks in my path? I keep them all. With them I shall build my castle."
—Nemonox

WHEN YOU INVEST, YOU ARE taking the extra money from your account and making it work for you. Investment options can be as simple as signing up for a 401(k), putting a few dollars into stocks and bonds or buying a few shares of a mutual fund. At its core, investing is the process of allowing someone else to use your money in return for a share of their profit. Your open investment accounts are considered your investment 'portfolio'. If you only have a company pension, that is what your entire portfolio consists of. Some may have a mix of stocks, bonds, mutual funds and IRAs, etc.

Risk is involved in every investment. The general rule of thumb is that the higher the risk, the greater the return. Though investing is not technically considered gambling, you do have the potential to lose your money. This is why careful consideration and deliberate planning are important; so, you can steadily grow your wealth and live comfortably on those investments.

Why Invest?

Life is unpredictable. You never know what's going to happen next, but you do know that it's most likely going to require money. Having funds set aside that are growing helps secure your financial future. Some are intimidated by investing because they don't understand it, don't know where to start or may not believe they'll ever have enough to invest. Then there are those who remember the stock market crashes and economic downturns where many people lost everything. All are very valid concerns, but not enough to keep you out of the game. As with anything, the stock market has its 'seasons' and it is based on what is going on in the world. You have to take the steps necessary to educate yourself on how it works so that you can benefit from the good (earning interest on your money) that it offers. No worries, you can learn bit by bit and I have outlined a primer to help—keep reading!

PORTFOLIO

Your open investment accounts are considered your 'portfolio'. It could be a mix of any investment option, stocks, bonds, mutual funds, CDs, etc.

**Mutual funds and retirement fund accounts are collections of stocks and bonds sold as packages, this is discussed more in the next section that outlines basic investing types.*

When Should I Add Investing to My Financial Life?

Investing is an advanced step in your financial plan. Answer these questions:

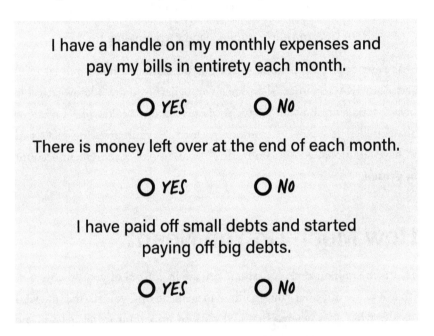

I have a handle on my monthly expenses and pay my bills in entirety each month.

O YES   O NO

There is money left over at the end of each month.

O YES   O NO

I have paid off small debts and started paying off big debts.

O YES   O NO

If you did not say Yes to all of these, you should postpone investing outside of your employer retirement account until you can. I don't believe you have to be out of debt before you begin investing, especially if you are 35 or older, but I do believe in getting on a solid financial ground first.

Where Do You Start?

Great investment strategies start with a plan. The plan depends on your age, how much money you have to invest, your financial goals and the level of risk you're willing to take.

Here is a suggested roadmap, again, tweak it based on your needs and disposable income, but this gives you an idea:

1. 401K Start here, once you are contributing at least 10–15% then…

2. Mutual Fund, once you have 1 or 2, add a

3. Roth IR A to your portfolio…and keep building from there.

As your disposable income increases, you can open more mutual fund and Roth IRA accounts. Then once you believe you are a knowledgeable investor, possibly buy some stocks via a discount broker like Etrade or Sharebuilder. It is key to continue to increase your investing goals and to have additional accounts outside of your employer retirement account or pension.

How Much Do You Need?

That is the million-dollar question. You are in control of your wealth and, while anyone can offer you wealth management tips, you are the one who decides what goes where. That's why it's so important to have a realistic picture of your current finances and to know what you're building wealth for. Begin with the end in mind and that will help you estimate how much you'll need. Do you want to supplement your retirement? Build a dream home one day? Start a business? Many want to pass money down to their children and grandchildren. Maybe you have a goal of being a millionaire one day. It is all achievable.

INVESTING ON A BUDGET

If you want to tip your toe in and start with a small amount of money just to apply what you are learning you can use a discount broker to open a brokerage account. Sound fancy? It's not a big deal, really. A brokerage account is simply an account that allows you to buy and sell investments. It's a little like opening a bank account, you're just doing it with a brokerage firm. Here, we are discussing online brokerage accounts that allow you to begin investing with very little money vs. traditional brokerage accounts.

Retirement accounts are also considered "brokerage" accounts; we discuss those in Chapter 12.

When you're going to need the money will determine the type of investment you choose. In other words, if you have 20 years, you may choose a type of IRA, whereas if you only have a couple of years, a mutual fund or CD may be better. Having these numbers at your disposal will also help you figure out how much you need to invest.

RISK: Don't Put All Your Eggs in One Basket

The best way to defer the potential risks of your investments is through diversification. I know, we hear about this all the time. It's no big deal really; it only means having more than one type of investment. Spreading your investments around in multiple areas gives you the cushion to brace yourself if one investment fails, you still have others that can support your financial goals. No matter how excellent an investment vehicle seems to be, there's always the chance that things can go awry, and you'll lose money.

Diversification Example 1:

Let's take Kevin for example, he is a nurse at a local hospital and has the following investment portfolio:

- Employer 401k

- Mutual fund focused on growth

- Stock in two tech companies

- Stock in one healthcare company

- 10 Bonds—many received as gifts

Diversification Example 2:

Another version of diversification is based on the stocks held in your mutual fund or retirement account. You don't want to have a mutual fund or retirement account that only invests in all tech stocks because if the technology industry fails, you will take a huge loss. Instead, you want to have a mix of various industries.

Craig has $3,000 to invest, which he saved from his tax return. He chose to put $2,000 in a mutual fund that represented various industries he was interested in. This fund included a balanced percentage of the following types of stocks:

technology   consumer staples

healthcare   financial services

If Craig were to put the entire $2,000 in a fund heavy in any one of those areas, he would lose money if that fund took a dip. Because he has diversified, his investment should remain stable. And the remaining $1,000? Since he already has an emergency fund, he opened an IRA separate from the 401(k) he has with his employer. His plan is to direct deposit $100 per month into both his IRA and his mutual fund.

So now when you hear the financial gurus on television talking about 'portfolio diversification', you know exactly what they are talking about!

Once you consider your risk, it's time to visit your financial advisor. This leads us to…

How to Choose a Financial Advisor

Financial advisors are needed and there are many who are excellent at their job. One way to find one for your finances is to ask family and friends for references. LinkedIn is also a good way to find professionals. Some advisors have free workshops or may be guest speakers in the community. I like these type of events because you can get to know them in a sense before doing business with them.

Pick at least three to five to consider and meet with each of them. Planners have to file an ADV Form Part II with the Securities and Exchange Commission (SEC) which shows their services, background, and fees. Most will automatically share this form with you, but if not, you can ask for it. States also have records on each financial advisor, you can check with the securities regulator in your state for complaints and to ensure they are licensed. Also, if they are a member of the National Association of Personal Financial Advisors (NAPFA) **www.napfa.org**, they don't receive commissions or other incentives for selling or recommending particular investment products.

Everyone who meets with a financial advisor should:

1. Have educated yourself on basic investing concepts like those found in this chapter

2. Know how much money you want to invest

3. Know what you want the advisor to do for you and be able to tell them

4. Ask for references

5. Have questions prepared, such as: how long have they been an advisor, what is their main area of focus, why are they suggesting a particular route for you, etc.

Pay attention to the advisor, are they listening to what you are saying your goals are, are they asking you questions about yourself or are they simply telling you what you should do or what they think is best. Don't get me wrong, they are there to advise you and you need be open to their suggestions. That said, they should be able to tell you clearly how their solutions line up with your stated goals. You should never feel pushed into a saving or investing direction you are not comfortable with.

Never buy at the first meeting. Go home, think about your options and then make a decision. Don't feel like you are bugging the advisor if you have to call with questions after the meeting, that is what they are there for and most don't mind.

Types of Accounts

Brokerage

A **traditional brokerage** account gives you access to the advice and expertise of a stockbroker. Companies like Edward Jones and UBS are traditional brokerage firms. Your broker will give you financial advice, portfolio reports and can be reached very easily. They will also offer research materials and explain them to help guide your investment decisions. These types of services can be very expensive and charge high commission rates, but if you're looking for the ease associated with having someone else handle your investment decisions, this is the way to go. This higher level of service also results in faster turn-around times for each trade. Most traditional brokerage accounts have minimum deposit requirements and charge fees on your account if it is below a certain amount. These fees will eat into your investments early on, especially if you're just beginning

Discount brokerage firms also have brokers, but they only handle the nuts and bolts of trades. There's generally an online system that account holders will use to buy and sell orders and the brokers on the other end handle the rest, no questions asked. It may be difficult to actually talk to a broker if you have one of these accounts. Because this type of service is more DIY (do it yourself), you pay significantly lower commissions. The amount of research and the tools available to discount brokerage account holders has been improving.

Certificates of Deposit

Certificates of Deposit are very secure investments in that you are guaranteed to get the amount you invested back plus interest once the CD matures. The interest rates are low though, maybe a little more than a money market or interest bearing checking or saving account. There are varying types of CD accounts and a visit to your local bank can help you determine which one may be right for you. *Types of CDs:*

Traditional

This is the original old school CD. You deposit a certain amount for a certain term and earn interest. If you withdraw before the term is up you will pay hefty penalties, but you are able to add money to the CD during the term.

Bump-up

If you buy a CD and then see the rate goes up, you can 'bump up' to that higher rate for the rest of your CDs term. Generally, you can do this once during the life of the CD.

Liquid

With this type you are able to withdraw without penalty, but the money must stay in the account at least 7 days. There may also be a limit on the number of withdrawals you can make. Of course the interest rate is lower than other CDs, that aren't so liquid.

Zero-coupon

A zero-coupon CD is bought at a discount, (think Groupon), but you are paid face value upon maturity. For example, you may pay $10,000 for a CD valued at $20,000. Though you don't earn interest on these type of CDS, you are paid the full value of $20,000 upon its maturity.

Individual Retirement Accounts (IRAs)

This type of account is perfect for those who aren't offered an employer plan, are looking to save more for retirement or want to follow my advice of stashing away money for retirement separate from your employer account. There are traditional IRAs (before tax contributions) and Roth IRAs (after-tax contributions) These are discussed in detail in Chapter 9 on retirement.

Your Employer

The easiest way to start investing is to participate in your employer-sponsored retirement account. This is often a 401(k), 403(b), 457 or governmental TSP account. These accounts generally use a combination of mutual funds, stocks, and bonds to spread out risk. While some employers have dropped this benefit since the economic downturn, many will still pay in matching funds at either a percentage or an equal match to what you contribute to the fund. Over time, your fund grows and doesn't get taxed until you withdraw your money. We talk about these types of accounts in depth in our Retirement Chapter 9.

Many like to have at least $1,000 when opening a brokerage account. But no worries if you'd like to start with less, most discount brokerages have no or low account minimum requirements.

Types of Investments

We've all heard triumphant stories about investors being at the right place at the right time and making millions in the market. We've also heard tragic stories about how investors have lost millions of dollars on bad investment decisions. For those of you who are new to investing, it can seem like a huge minefield of good and bad decisions and opinions. While there are risks in making investments, it's still an opportunity to prepare for your future and set yourself up for life. There are a number of ways to invest, and you can start small and slow to ease into it.

Bonds

Government bonds (including federal, state, and local) and corporate bonds (from large companies) are considered safe investments when compared to stocks and mutual funds. The entity that issues bonds asks for your investment. In return for your investment, the bonds offer you a small amount of guaranteed interest after a certain period of time. You might receive a one-year bond at 1% from a company. That company is guaranteeing that when the bond matures, it will give you your investment back, plus 1%. The percentage rates on bonds are usually very low because the issuing entity cannot predict the movement of the market and other areas, and doesn't know exactly how much interest it will really earn on its investments.

Stocks

Over the last 85 years, stocks have generally outperformed most other investment alternatives. According to Ibbotson Associates, an institutional investment advisory firm, stocks have gone up an average of 10.4% over the past 90 years. When you purchase a stock, what you're doing is purchasing a very small piece of ownership in a particular company. As stocks are traded back and forth, the market decides just how much each piece of stock is worth that day. To purchase stocks, an investor will almost always work through a brokerage firm.

Before deciding which stocks to buy, consider how risk averse you are and how much time you have to hold on to the investment. If you are very risk averse, going with long-term, proven stocks, such as utilities and other large, well-established corporations, are your best bet. If you're after potentially larger and quicker profits in your investment portfolio, then riskier stocks in rapid growth areas may be right for you.

Mutual Funds

Instead of owning a single stock or bond, mutual funds are collections of stocks and bonds sold as packages. Investors mutually pool their money and invest in shares of this fund. The money made from mutual funds is then redistributed in the form of dividends based on the amount of money that was put into the fund.

DIVIDENDS

If an investment earns a certain amount of profit, some of that profit (cash) is then paid out to the shareholders quarterly or annually.

One of the largest advantages this type of investment offers is a lower cost per entry. Since a mutual fund pools together money from various sources, one person doesn't have to carry the entire load of the mutual fund itself. It's diversified to the point where there's not as much risk involved.

There are costs associated with the administration and management of a mutual fund that we will discuss later. Costs are added because there are a lot of moving parts within a fund. Did you know that someone still has to purchase the individual securities and bonds and then make the separate investment to group all of them together?

Where to Open an Account

1. **Brokerage Firm**—facilitates the purchase of all investments

2. **Financial Advisor**—works with a brokerage firm to purchase your investments

3. **Banks**—works with a brokerage firm the same as a financial advisor would

4. **Directly**—you can buy investments directly, but this is suggested for the savvy investor only. Beginning investors should get professional help when purchasing until they are more knowledgeable and have done extensive research

There are a lot of good brokerage firms out there and it is becoming more and more popular to purchase via a discount online brokerage firm. Now they are called discount because there are less fees, but also remember you won't receive those gold amenities either. Many are okay with this because they feel they are getting a bigger bang for their buck. Every time you make a trade there's normally some sort of fee that goes along with it, but you aren't paying as much as you do with traditional brokerage firms. Here are some of the most popular and their terms/fees as of the writing of this book:

- **E* Trade:** E*Trade was one of the first online brokerages to offer every type of investment and they're still a market leader. They require no account minimums and charge no account service fees. E*Trade charges a standard $9.99 per stock and options trade with varying rates for other investments. They also offer a full suite of research tools at no cost.

- **Sharebuilder:** Sharebuilder tries to distinguish itself as the lowest cost choice for long-term buy-and-hold investors. This is because they offer an automated investing plan with commissions of only $4 per trade. They also have no account minimums and charge no service fees. However, if you decide to change investments or invest outside the automated plan, you'll pay $9.95 per trade. Sharebuilder also offers research tools, but not as many as E*Trade.

- **Fidelity:** Fidelity was initially only a full-service brokerage but has grown to become an online leader over the last few years. They offer every type of account and investment, but many people opt for their traditional accounts and low prices. There are no annual fees if you maintain an account minimum of $2,500 and their minimum deposit requirement is $2,500 for most accounts. They also have a standard $7.95 commission on all stock trades.

When opening a brokerage account, it's always best to investigate all of your options and match your investment strategy to the level of interaction you wish to have with the account. These discount options are very good if you want to try your hand at doing the research and making the investments yourself. But a full-service brokerage or a financial advisor might be the best choice if you don't wish to be concerned with the day-to-day movement of your money.

HOW TO RESEARCH COMPANIES TO INVEST IN

We discussed that mutual funds and stocks all have 'ticker' symbols; you can research their historical and projected performance on financial websites such as Morningstar and Yahoo Finance.

In addition to researching how much money they may make you, you will also want to check for any negative or positive media about company stock or mutual fund.

Is the CEO in the media?

Has there been any product recalls or other happenings that may cause stock price to dip? You will want a mutual fund that has had consistent returns of 8 -12% over an 8–12 year period. Choose one where the fund manager has been in place for 10 years or more.

You can research the types of industries and companies that are in your mutual fund accounts to determine if there are any current events that may affect the funds' performance as well.

DO THIS ACTION STEPS
Ask Yourself a Few Questions

There are a few things to consider when deciding where to invest:

1. Grab your investing cheat sheet here:
   dorethiakelly.com/moneychathub

2. What are you comfortable with? Are you generally more conservative or are you willing to bet the farm?

3. How much money can you afford to lose without losing sleep? There's nothing wrong with taking risks as long as you understand your limits and know when to make adjustments. If you watch every penny, you may want to opt for safer investments that grow income slower.

4. Based on your age and when you'll need to access your money, what is the best mix of investments for you? A younger person can generally take more risks because they have more time to accumulate wealth.

SAY THIS #MONEYCHAT MANTRAS

" *I am not afraid to invest*

" *I invest wisely*

" *I'm educating myself on investing strategies so I can build wealth*

Wait a Minute. We are Talking about Investing. What about Annuities?

Annuities are investment vehicles that provide a guaranteed payment for a specific period of time, i.e., 10 to 20 years or the rest of your life. To put it in perspective, we're all familiar with social security and pensions, right? Well, those are also types of annuities—they're just offered by the government or your employer. Individuals can also buy their own annuity from an investment advisor or insurance company.

FIXED ANNUITIES

Fixed annuities give you fixed payments over the life (time frame) of the annuity. In the case of the social security system or the pension system, that fixed payment amount is dependent upon the amount of money you've put in and your expected lifespan. (Insurance people have amazingly detailed tables to determine this information.)

Let's say you have $50,000 to put into an annuity, and you want to get an annuity that will give you a payment for the rest of your life, which you expect to be 15 more years. You would buy a 15-year annuity that would give you around $277 each month.

The math:

$50,000/15 years = $3,333 per year

$3,333/12 months = $277.00 per month

VARIABLE ANNUITIES

Variable annuities give you fluctuating payments over the life of the annuity. Payments amounts are based on the investments inside the annuity, your expected lifespan, and how much money you have invested.

For example, if you put that same $50,000 in a variable annuity, you would receive your $277 as a minimum, but it could also be more since payments fluctuate.

GUARANTEED ANNUITIES

There is often concern over what happens to an annuity in case you die. A guaranteed annuity ensures payouts even in the event of the annuity owner's death. Payments would go to your estate.

JOINT ANNUITIES

Joint annuities can be passed on from person to person in the event of your death. This works in cases where you want to make sure your spouse is "taken care of" on your passing. Usually, the payments are lower, but a guaranteed payment is still being made.

PROS AND CONS OF INVESTING IN ANNUITIES

PROS

The biggest incentive to setting up an annuity is the automatic payments you receive each month for the rest of your life. This provides a budgeting foundation and gives you a little more peace of mind. This is key during retirement years or in the case of a medical concern that doesn't allow you to work.

If you haven't quite gotten a handle on your financial habits, the money is out of your hands with no opportunity to blow it and have nothing to show for it later.

CONS

Before establishing a personal annuity, make sure that it is the right investment vehicle for you. Once you've invested in an annuity, it's nearly impossible to withdraw the money—annuities are designed to be irrevocable. Getting your money back usually involves very costly surrender charges.

The money you receive from your annuity is also not adjusted for inflation. Two hundred dollars now may be great, but that same amount 10 years from now might only get you a stick of gum.

There is also a cost for setting up and administering the annuity. In many cases, you can pay up to two to three percent of the value of your investment every year. These payments drive down the overall value of the investment.

As with any investment, do your homework before choosing an annuity and talk with your financial advisor or insurance agent to discuss your options.

CHAPTER 10

Investing 102: Diving In

#MoneyChat

"You don't have to be a genius to invest well."
—Warren Buffet

OF COURSE, I COULDN'T WRITE about investing and not quote Warren Buffet! I like this quote because I believe it wholeheartedly. Take baby steps, learn the rules, and win the game!

Class is in session! Throughout this chapter, I will be telling you to do your homework, to do your research, at the end of it I tell you how!

Here we will take a deep dive—equipping you with the information needed to invest wisely!

Micro Investing Explained

If someone told you that you should start investing, the first thing you might think about is how much money you'd need to make this happen.

When you think of investing or investors, don't just picture a someone super wealthy who has a lot of extra money to part with.

Everyday people like you and me can find the money to invest and it's important that you do. Investing is one of the best ways to grow your money over time and ensure you'll have enough during **retirement**. One of the best ways to get started is with micro investing.

Just as the name suggests, micro investing allows you to start investing on much smaller terms. Normally, when you invest in stocks you buy shares of the company which gives you a portion of ownership.

When that company does well and interest on your investment compounds, you get paid dividends. What may sound intimidating is the price to buy certain stocks. To buy a single share of Google as of this writing you'd need to spend $1,605. A share of Amazon stock is even higher.

Of course, there are lower priced stocks but an alternative option most people are considering to help them get started is **buying fractional shares or "pieces" of a stock.**

Buying fractional shares means you're purchasing a piece of a stock, so this lowers your cost. For example, a share of Nike stock costs around $91.84 right now. You can buy Nike for even less than that by purchasing a fractional share. That way, you can get started and grow your investments over time as you can afford to contribute more money to building your portfolio.

Micro investing apps make it super easy to start investing with as little as

$5. Sure, it's not much but it's better than nothing and helps you get started instead of pushing it off. Here are some of the best micro investing apps to consider using.

**If you are using any of these apps or similar, you have been micro investing already, but maybe didn't have a name for it!*

Acorns is a great micro investing apps because it helps you invest your spare change. Most of at least a few dollars that we can spare each day, but it often gets lost on small purchases or the coins just sit in the cup holder in our car.

You could be investing this money instead and seeing it add up and grow over time. Acorns has monthly plans that range from $1 to $3 so it's pretty affordable. You can also set up regular weekly transfers to boost your savings. Just like any other investment, your balance can grow with compound interest.

Stash is another micro investing app that actually allows you to start investing with stocks, ETFs and bonds. You can get started with just $5. Stash also provides guides on investing which is helpful, and you can set up automatic transfers from your checking account. Stash does cost between $1–$9 per month to use.

Stockpile allows you to choose from thousands of fractional shares of stocks and ETFs. It's free to sign up and only costs $0.99 per trade.

What's great about Stockpile is that you can also buy stock gift cards for your family, friends, and your kids.

What I love about micro investing is that it removes the "I don't have enough money to invest" barrier…. ahem… excuse. It doesn't take much money at all.

A mistake I see many people doing is signing up for an account and blindly allocating money. It's like closing your eyes and spinning the wheel hoping for a good outcome. You still want to understand investing and how it works. Most of these sites also have an education section where people can learn how to invest, but many do not take the time to read the information.

Another thing, if you set up a retirement account through one of these companies the same rules apply as if you did it on your own or through your employer. There are still taxes and penalties if you withdraw early.

Stocks

When people think of investing, the first thing that probably comes to mind is a stock. The state of the stock market is a daily news item and the Dow Jones Industrial Average (aka DJIA or The DOW) is an accepted barometer of how well the economy is doing.

While the market is complex, the basics are simple. A single share of stock represents the smallest amount of ownership you can have in a company and when you buy a stock, you're buying a very tiny portion of the company. People with a lot of stock in a company can influence it through shareholder meetings, but that will come later. What's more important to know at this point is how stocks make money for you. There are two main methods.

Buy Low/Sell High

The first method is buying a stock when its price is low and selling it when its price is high. To look up the cost of a stock or, to use investing terminology, its *share price*, you'll need to find out two things:

- Which *exchange* the stock is traded on

- The stock's *ticker symbol*. This can be searched for at **www.finance.yahoo.com**

- When you look at the newspaper listings for a stock, you'll normally get three pieces of information:

- The price of the stock at the end of the trading day before

- The amount by which its price went up or down over the course of that day

- The percent by which its price has changed

Looking at Amazon as I write this, I see that it's trading at $254.23 and that it's down $3.85, or 1.51%. But that's just its relative change during the day. Stocks are really a long-term game. Most people suggest holding on to a share of stock for about two to three years before trying to sell it off.

Amazon is traded on the NASDAQ exchange and its ticker symbol is AMZN. Over a five-day spread, a share of Amazon stock rose from

$249.27 to $258.05. So, if you bought a single share of stock on the first day of the five-day spread and sold it four days later, you would have made $8.78 ($258.05–$249.27). This may not seem like much and you're right. However, if you bought this share of Amazon stock way back in May of 2008 when its price was $77.31, selling it at the end of our five-day spread would have yielded $180.74. That's not a bad return *and* that's only one share!

Now if the stock had gone in the other direction, you would have lost money when you sold it. This is why investing is a calculated risk. Do you sell off the stock now and eat your loss before its price goes down any further, or do you hold on to it and pray that its price goes up again, and that it goes up enough to make it profitable? This is why you must research companies before you buy their stock; so, you can judge whether or not they'll be profitable over time. Companies that report regular profits and growth in their quarterly earnings reports are seen as more valuable, and this pushes the stock price up. Companies that don't perform as well in their quarterly earnings are somewhat devalued and their stock's price goes down. This is why earnings reports are so eagerly reported in financial news.

> **EARNINGS REPORTS** are simply financial reports companies publish quarterly to show how strong their company is financially. Did they make a profit? If so, how much? If not, why and do they expect to do better next quarter?

By spreading your investment capital (money) over multiple stocks, you can absorb price fluctuations a lot easier. "Blue chip" stocks make a great first investment in the stock market. These are the stocks of companies that are very well established and are very unlikely to collapse, though nothing's impossible.

Dividends

The other way that stocks make money for you is through dividends. When a company makes a profit, it can decide to pay some of that profit directly to its shareholders. The amount you get depends on how much stock you own, how much stock is out there for that company, and how much of the profit the shareholders vote to pay out as dividends. Some companies pay quarterly dividends, others yearly and some not at all. For most beginning investors, dividends are a sort of bonus that happens on occasion.

Mutual Funds

One of the problems with diversification is a lack of capital… aka cash! Many beginning investors aren't able to spread out their money enough to be safe in investing. Mutual funds came about as a way to get around this problem. In a mutual fund, your money is pooled with other people's money. The company managing the fund then invests that money into many different kinds of investments.

If you have any sort of retirement account, like a 401(k) or a Roth IRA, you probably have investments in one or more mutual funds already. When you look over the different "plans" you can invest in through a 401(k), most of them are mutual funds of one kind or another. When you invest in a mutual fund, you get shares—much like stock—that signify what portion of the holdings in the fund belong to you.

How do you earn money from mutual funds?

- Dividends on stocks and interest on bonds

- Selling investments the fund holds that have increased in price

- The shares of the mutual fund themselves increase in price, which can then be sold by you

Now, you can receive a check for the money earned or you have the option to reinvest to buy more shares. The latter is the suggested strategy; remember investing should be a long-term journey. You cut yourself short if you cash in earnings.

The advantages of a mutual fund are ease of diversification and their *liquidity* (how easy it is to access your money). You are able to close the account and pocket your money whenever you choose without any penalties.

Alright, hold on tight—there are many different types of mutual funds:

- Money market funds invest in *short-term debt instruments*. These are very safe. You can't lose your *principal* (initial investment) with these. However, their rate of return is very low, about as good as a certificate of deposit (CD).

- **Bond funds**—The goal of these funds is to provide a steady income to all their investors through investing in the bond market. These are great for conservative investors, but there's still risk involved and you are subject to bond interest rate fluctuations.

- **Equity funds (Stocks)**—This is the largest category of mutual funds; they invest in stocks and are divided into 'classes' dependent on:

  1. The size of the company (small, mid-size or large) in terms of how much capital (money) they have.

  2. How risky those companies' investments are (value, growth, or blend).

     a. Value—may be undervalued in that the stock may be trading at a lower price than the company is actually worth. Focus is on safety rather than growth, so the investing strategy is not as aggressive.

     b. Growth—riskier, but also have better returns, these companies are expected to have faster growth and earnings potential than others.

     c. Blend—you guessed it, a combination of the two.

- **Balanced funds**—are a mix of stocks and bonds, the idea is provide some level of safety and income diversifying the two types of investments.

- **Global or International funds**—At first glance, you would think these meant the same thing, right? Nope. A global fund invests in foreign stocks that do not include your home country. International funds invest in foreign stocks, but could include your home country. Some are wary of investing in foreign stocks, but you just have to do your homework as with anything else. You will face risks based on the country, politics, etc., but do your research. These types of funds are good for diversifying your portfolio and depending on the countries represented, may provide the returns you desire.

- **Index Funds**—Invests in companies based on the market indexes such as Standard & Poors (S&P) 500 or Dow Jones Industrial Average (DJIA). These funds have lower fees than regular mutual funds and you don't have to pay brokerage commissions.

- **Exchange Traded Funds**—Also follows the indexes, trades like regular stock on an exchange and you have to pay brokerage commissions. Prices fluctuate throughout the day as they are bought and sold.

- **Specialty Funds**—Invests in companies within the same: Sector— technology, healthcare, finance, etc.

  Region—certain countries or geographical areas

  Socially responsible—may not invest in things that are against beliefs such as alcohol, weapons, cigarettes, etc.

Mutual Fund Fees

Of course, the people running the funds need to eat and so there are fees involved with mutual funds. There are two main types of fees: a *MER* and a *load*.

Management Expense Ratio (MER), is the fee for managing the fund and is calculated as a percentage of the fund's assets. The average rate is between 0.2% and 1.5%. Higher fees don't necessarily mean that you'll get a better rate on return. Unfortunately, this is the price you pay in the mutual fund game and you'll have to watch your statements carefully to make sure you're getting a good return on your mutual fund investment.

Loads are fees taken from you to pay the salespeople for selling you the fund. It's basically their commission. The beginning investor should avoid any fund with a load. There are plenty of no-load (no fee) mutual funds and they often out-perform those with fees.

When you go to a broker, a bank or a mutual fund website, you'll need to know a few things.

Net Asset Value (NAV), of the mutual fund. This is how much you'll need to pay to buy a share in the fund. It's much like the share price of a stock.

Second, you should know how much risk you're willing to endure, how much money you want to invest and whether you want to do it all at once or over time. All of this information will help your financial planner decide which funds to show you.

You can also use a service like Morningstar.com to help search through funds and get their rankings and current information about them. In fact, the Internet is the best place to learn about funds now. You can get a long-term analysis of a fund to see its performance over time, which will be the best thing for an initial investor. Save day trading for the experts who can stomach it!

CAPITAL GAINS TAXES!

You will have to pay taxes on the dividends you receive at the end of the year. Talk to an accountant and a financial advisor about capital gains taxes and your mutual fund investments.

Whew! Okay, take a deep breath. I know it is a lot to take in, but you are doing fine! Next, we're going to dip into the last major area of investing—the bond market.

Bonds

Compared to the exciting volatility of the stock market, bonds may seem boring. However, bonds are an extremely important part of the economy and a safe place to put your money long term if you do it correctly.

First, a bond is basically an I.O.U. If a corporation or government wants to fund operations or a special project, they can issue bonds to the public. Let's say you buy a $1,000 bond. One thousand dollars is the bond's *face value*. In exchange for your $1,000, the company issuing the bond (the *issuer*) promises to pay you yearly interest on it. This yearly interest is known as the *coupon*. The bond will pay interest until the length of the loan is up and the bond matures. The day this happens is called the *maturity date*. On that day, the issuer repays the investor the face value of the bond.

For example, if you buy a $5,000 bond at a 5% coupon for 10 years, you will receive $250 a year from the bond for 10 years, generally divided into two payments. At the end of 10 years, you'll get your

$5,000 back and you'll have made a profit of $2,500 dollars.

The major difference between bonds and stocks is that bonds are considered debt for the issuer. If the issuer was to go belly up, the bondholders would get paid first from any liquidation. But with a bond you don't get any share of company ownership like you would with a stock. Nor would you get any additional benefits if the company did very well from your investment. Thus, bonds have a lower return than stocks in most instances.

Many retirees love bonds because their principal is secure no matter what happens. Bonds are a great way to provide a fixed income. They're also very good if you have a short-term goal that must have a stable source of income, such as education.

The risk from bonds comes from the creditworthiness of the company issuing them. It's just like any other loan. Can you expect the company to pay back the face value and all the interest owed when the bond matures? Credit rating companies like Moody's and Fitch also rate the worthiness of bonds to show investors how good (or bad) the credit of a company is. A company whose bonds have a very low rating (called junk bonds) is much riskier to invest in, but you can get a very high coupon out of them. So-called *junk bonds* can be riskier than stocks.

Bonds come in several categories:

- *Bills* are bonds that mature in less than a year.

- *T-Notes (aka Notes)* are bonds that mature between two and 10 years.

- *Bonds* (true bonds) mature after 10 years or longer.

Bonds also differ by who issues them. U.S. government bonds are issued in all the types above, and are normally called T-bills/notes/bonds, short for Treasury. Because the U.S. is so stable, Treasury bonds are some of the safest investments out there. However, developing countries also issue bonds to fund infrastructure products and there's a lot of risk there. As recent financial crises have shown, countries can default just like companies can.

The cost for investing in Treasury securities is quite low. But the lower you go, the fewer advantages you have. The normal minimum price you have to purchase to get a Treasury security is $1,000. However, there are special Savings Bonds that can be bought at lower rates and have a coupon! The two current types are EE Series bonds and I Series bonds. The minimum purchase price for these is $25 and you can buy up to $10,000 per social security number per year. You have to hold them for at least a year before you can cash them out. They must also be bought through TreasuryDirect.gov. For more information on Savings Bonds, check out **www.treasurydirect.gov/indiv/research/indepth/ebonds/res_e_bonds_eecomparison.htm**. If you're not ready to do major investing in standard Treasury securities then Savings Bonds are the way to go.

Municipal bonds are those issued by city governments allowing you to invest in that city. Depending on your bond and your relationship with the city, some of these bonds are tax-free. Municipal bonds can provide a significant savings on your investment. It is more likely that a city will go bankrupt before the federal government, but it would still be pretty rare. And, finally, there are corporate bonds, which are issued by companies. These have the highest yields because they're the most prone to risk. The normal minimum amount you need to purchase to get one is $5,000.

There are lower-priced options that have no coupon. Instead, you pay a cost lower than the face cost of the bond and get the full price of it at a later date. These are known as zero-coupon bonds, discount bonds, or deep discount bonds. These are not good for investment, but they are excellent if you need a specific amount of income at a later date. For example, if you know you want to have a certain amount of money for college for your child, you could by zero-coupon bonds. That way you wouldn't have to worry about fluctuating interest rates. Within the bond market, sometimes also called the debt market, the credit market, or the fixed income market, you have two different types of purchasers. There's the market between the investors and the issuers, and there's the market made of people who are trading bonds back and forth among themselves.

If you want more information on bonds, I highly recommend this comprehensive page from Investopedia http://www.investopedia.com/university/bonds. Everything is explained in an easy-to-understand manner.

To buy a bond, just talk with any broker. Remember that you may need to meet minimum investment amounts to buy certain types of loans. You can also buy bonds directly from the issuer, especially government bonds. Remember, you can buy U.S. government bonds at **www.treasurydirect. gov**, which will have all the info you need to buy T-notes, T-bills, T-bonds, and savings bonds.

Key Points:

- Buying a bond is like giving a loan to the government or municipality. When it matures, or when you cash it in in the case of a savings bond, you get your principle (face value) plus interest (coupon payments) back.

- They are a very stable investment option. In fact, Treasury securities are considered to be one of the most stable investment options in the world.

- Treasury securities require a $1000 minimum investment. Municipal bonds require a $5000 minimum investment.

- Savings bonds (types EE and I) can be bought for as little as $25 each.

- To buy bonds, talk with a broker or go to TreasuryDirect.gov.

- Some bonds have no coupon. That means you pay a discount on the face value of the bond, then get the face value of the bond back at a later date. Not good for investing, but good for things like college tuition.

- Take the short Investopedia course mentioned above to get a deeper insight into the specifics of buying and trading bonds.

Before We Say "I Do:" Couples and Investing

Financial Expert—La Keisha Mallet

We are currently living in an age where being financially astute should be a way of life for all of us. Times have changed, dynamics in the home have changed and, many times, both partners in a relationship work outside of the home, just to make ends meet. Getting married, planning a wedding, and deciding to share the rest of your life with the one you love is probably one of the most joyous occasions in a person's life. Finding that special someone and vowing to commit the rest of your life to loving and cherishing them, 'til death do you part, is not a task anyone should take lightly.

With fights about money and money problems being the number one cause of divorce, many couples get married not knowing that debt is a key destructive force that has ruined many marriages. Having a heart-to-heart discussion with the one you love about the state of your finances, and even your financial expectations, is not as sexy a topic as most lovers want to discuss, but I believe that if the hard financial questions are addressed before the nuptials, it will increase a couples' odds of 'til death do us part instead of 'til debt do us part.

Before I decided to say, "I do," I wanted to fully understand my partner's views on money, debt, savings, retirement, etc. I wanted to know if he had any financial goals and if any of his goals were aligned with things that were also important to me. One of the first questions I chose to ask my future husband was, "What drives your decisions with money?" And there were books that helped us engage in healthy communication concerning our current financial situations. One of those books was *The Hard Questions: 100 Questions to Ask Before Getting Engaged* by Susan Piver.

The Hard Questions addressed many of the necessary topics a couple should discuss in any premarital session. It urged couples to discuss the expectations they had for their marriage, to examine how those expectations differed and to find some common ground regarding those differences. Topics included things like where to live, whether to have children or adopt, how close is too close for the in-laws and, of course, the topic dearest to me— *money*. The book gave detailed questions to ask your potential spouse about how they viewed money and I used those questions to help determine whether Jeff and I would thrive together financially. I asked Jeff questions like how much debt he had and if there was a plan to pay it off. That question was easy for me to answer because I had achieved debt freedom early in our dating relationship. I also asked him whether his dream home was in the big city or the suburbs. Was sending his children to private school an option—from a financial perspective? Or would public education be the best choice? We went on to discuss how much money we each had in our checking and savings accounts and if we were aggressively stashing cash for a rainy day.

From there the conversation turned to investing. We discussed our investing philosophies and I discovered that I'm more of a conservative investor while Jeff has his own brokerage accounts and is quite an aggressive investor. At this realization, we decided that after the wedding we would continue to invest as we had but create a joint portfolio that would be a mix of our different investing styles.

As we coach couples about money, we always stress the importance of being on the same page and being in agreement. No two people are exactly alike, and neither will their philosophies on money and investing be. It's vital that each partner voices their needs from a personal finance perspective and is clear about what their financial goals are and how they wish to achieve them.

My husband likes to dabble in day trading. I think it's too risky and not a wise investment move. However, outside of our savings and the investments we share, and after we take care of all of our responsibilities, any money left over goes to Jeff for him to invest. That was important for us to decide in advance so that in the event Jeff's stocks don't perform as well as he hopes, I won't have to give him the evil eye for blowing money we need. We urge each partner to understand their risk tolerance level and the role it will play in their approach to investing as a married couple. It's so important for couples to learn to communicate their financial desires and plans long before they decide on wedding colors, caterers, and flowers.

I believe all couples should have "the talk"—how to invest, when to invest and where to invest (outside of 401(k)s and IRAs). The couples we coach often wonder if they should have joint investments. While that's a personal preference, I'm a firm believer in the art of communication. Each spouse is responsible for understanding the financial affairs of the unit and for being aware of how the money in every account is changing from month to month each quarter. Couples must also reach a mutual agreement as to when it is necessary to increase the amount they invest.

With regard to buying stocks, another decision couples need to make is when to buy, sell and hold. There will likely be times when one partner wants to buy and the other wants to sell. There has to have been a discussion about how to handle situations when you disagree about money. This strategy works for other areas in the relationship as well. When discussing any piece of the financial equation with your partner, only do what you feel comfortable doing because you have to be able to sleep at night. If investing 75% of your retirement account in stocks will cause you anxiety, then opt for a more conservative investment strategy. Whatever you decide, you have to be comfortable with the decision.

Once a couple has decided to marry their finances, it's imperative that they discuss when and for what reasons they will ever touch their invested money. I don't believe couples should touch their retirement savings for any reason, especially not to make major purchases. The penalties for withdrawing funds prematurely are too high. However, we do advise couples to have a particular fund that they regularly contribute to; an interest-bearing account that eventually will grow to a point where they can live off its interest.

After debt has been eliminated and long-term savings are in place, we advise our clients to save 10% of their take-home pay each month to put toward an "in case we need it" account. I like the term "in case we need it" for things that are not necessarily an emergency but are still unexpected or unanticipated.

Help your spouse stay on track with their financial goals. Make it fun and make it rewarding. When you reach a goal or major financial milestone, celebrate! Making money and watching it grow should be fun and easy. Take the stress out of discussing money by approaching it as equal partners who will one day enjoy the fruits of your joint labor. Who better to enjoy life on the beaches of the world with than your spouse? By talking about your finances early and often, you'll eventually have the money to do it.

CHAPTER 11

The Beginner's Guide to Crypto

#MoneyChat

HAVE YOU BEEN HEARING ABOUT cryptocurrency but don't know where to start? You're not alone. Cryptocurrency can be a confusing and intimidating topic for beginners. But it doesn't have to be! Not with this crash course in the basics I have for you. By the end, you'll know what cryptocurrency is, how it works, and whether or not it's something you should invest in. Let's get started!

Now, there was absolutely no way I could add even all the basic information about Crypto in a few pages. So, I have a full section about all things crypto at **dorethiakelly.com/crypto.** We will make sure it's always updated with all the latest information, definitions and changes you need to know.

What is Cryptocurrency?

In a nutshell, cryptocurrency is a digital or virtual asset designed to work as a medium of exchange. Cryptocurrencies are decentralized, which means they aren't subject to government or financial institution control. Bitcoin, the first and most well-known cryptocurrency, was created in 2009. Since then, thousands of other cryptocurrencies, and assets like crypto commodities and tokens have been created.

How Does Cryptocurrency Work?

Without delving too deeply into the mechanics behind cryptocurrency, it's helpful for you to know a few of the key concepts. Cryptocurrencies use encryption and blockchain technology to facilitate secure, peer-to-peer transactions. A blockchain is a shared database or digital ledger. It's decentralized, which means it is not subject to government or financial institution control. It's distributed, so transactions are verified across a vast network of computers. It's also immutable, so the data entered is permanent and irreversible.

How do Bitcoin nodes validate transactions? The nodes solve complex mathematical problems, and the first node to solve the problem gets to add the next "block" to the blockchain and is rewarded with cryptocurrency. This validation and reward process is known as "mining."

What Are Alt Coins?

When most people think of cryptocurrency, they think of Bitcoin. But Bitcoin is just one type of cryptocurrency, and it's not even the most popular one. In fact, there are thousands of different types of cryptocurrencies, commonly known as "alt" coins, which is an abbreviation for the word alternative. Alt coins are simply any type of cryptocurrency, or alternative, that isn't Bitcoin. That's all there is to it! There are alt coins for all sorts of different purposes, with different strengths and weaknesses. Popular alt coins include Ethereum, Ripple, Litecoin and Monero.

"Alt coins are simply any type of cryptocurrency, or alternative, that isn't Bitcoin."

Why Invest in Alt Coins?

Alt coins offer investors a number of advantages over Bitcoin. First of all, because there are so many different types of alt coins with different purposes, there's bound to be one that appeals to you more than others. Secondly, alt coins are often much cheaper than Bitcoin, so you can get more bang for your buck. Finally, some alt coins offer faster transaction times and lower fees than Bitcoin—making them more practical for day-to-day use.

When to Use Cryptocurrency

As the name suggests, cryptocurrency can be used to purchase goods and services just like any other currency. However, there are a few things to keep in mind when using cryptocurrency. First, because cryptocurrency is not regulated by governments or financial institutions, it is very volatile. This means that the value of cryptocurrency can change rapidly and unexpectedly. Second, because blockchain technology is still new and evolving, there are some security risks associated with using cryptocurrency. That being said, if you take precautions and **do your own research (DYOR),** you can use cryptocurrency safely and securely.

How to Use Cryptocurrency

To purchase, store, use or send cryptocurrency, you'll need to set up a digital wallet. A digital wallet is like a bank account for your cryptocurrency.

There are many different types of digital wallets, and which one you choose will depend on your needs and preferences. Once you download and set up your digital wallet, you can buy, sell, or trade cryptocurrency on a cryptocurrency exchange. These online platforms enable you to buy and sell cryptocurrency using fiat currency (i.e., government-issued paper money like USD or EUR).

"Fiat currency = paper money, coins"

Should I Invest in Cryptocurrency?

Now that you know what cryptocurrency is and how it works, you might be wondering if you should invest in it. There are pros and cons to investing in any asset, and cryptocurrency is no different. Some people believe that cryptocurrency is the future of money, while others think it's nothing more than a fad. Ultimately, whether or not you invest in cryptocurrency is up to you and should be based on your own research and financial goals. As a highly-volatile asset, investors are encouraged to diversify and balance their portfolio to match your lifestage and risk tolerance. Just like any investment, Cryptocurrency is something you invest in once you are set financially and you definitely want to take your time to learn it. Don't be in a hurry, but bit by bit understand what it is and how it works.

Psst… if you are still a lil' confused, keep reading, I've included a quick and dirty cheat sheet in the next few pages to help you visualize how it works. Of course, don't forget to visit **dorethiakelly.com/crypto** as well.

How to Buy Cryptocurrency

Alright, so now that you have a basic understanding you may be wondering where to get cryptocurrency. Here are five steps you need to take.

1. Choose a Cryptocurrency Exchange

A cryptocurrency exchange is a platform where you can buy, sell, or trade cryptocurrencies for other digital assets or traditional currencies like dollars or Euros. Some exchanges only work with certain types of cryptocurrencies, so it's important to do your own research (DYOR) to find an exchange that works with the type of currency you want to trade. Some popular exchanges for beginners include Gemini, Kraken, Crypto.com, and Coinbase.

2. Create an Account on the Exchange

Now that you've chosen an exchange, you'll need to create an account. This usually involves providing your personal information like your name and email address. You may also be required to provide additional information like your phone number or proof of ID. Once you've created an account, you'll need to deposit money into it so you can start trading.

3. Start Trading

With money in your account, you can start trading! To buy a cryptocurrency, select the amount you want and click "Buy." The funds will be taken from your account and converted into the currency you selected. To sell currency, select the amount you want and click "Sell." The funds will be converted back into your account currency. Most exchanges charge fees for each transaction. These fees can vary depending on the exchange platform, but generally are around one percent.

4. Withdraw Your Currency

If you want to cash out and convert your cryptocurrency back into fiat currency (paper money, i.e.: dollars), most exchanges will allow you to do this. However, there may be fees associated with withdrawing money from your account. Once you've withdrawn your currency, it is sent to the wallet of your choice.

5. Keep Track of Your Investments

It's important to keep track of how much money you put into each investment as well as how much money (if any) you make from each investment. Many people use Excel spreadsheets or other tracking methods but do consider using dynamic apps like CoinmarketCap or Blockfolio that track profits, losses, and portfolio valuations.

Who Crypto is and IS NOT For

Getting started with cryptocurrency can seem daunting but it doesn't have to be! By following these simple steps, you will get a grasp on buying and selling cryptocurrency when you are ready. Just remember to do your own research (DYOR) before getting started and always keep track of your investments! Below is a guideline you can use as just one way to determine if you are ready for crypto.

CRYPTO IS FOR YOU IF	CRYPTO IS **NOT** FOR YOU IF
You can make a little time each week to learn about how it works.	You don't understand what it is or how it works and don't have time to learn.
You don't mind risk—it's a volatile currency.	You don't already have emergency and retirement savings—focus there first for at least a year or two.
Most importantly, you are already on solid financial ground and can afford to lose the money you invest. Essentially, you have money to play with.	You have trouble paying your bills each month or several months out of the year.

HOW DOES
BLOCKCHAIN
WORK

 A transaction is requested

 The transaction is broadcasted to a network of nodes

 The network validates the transaction using known algorithms

VALIDATION MAY INCLUDE

 SMART CONTRACTS

 CRYPTOCURRENCY

 OTHER RECORDS

 The transaction is unified with other transactions as a block of data.

 The new block is added to the blockchain in a transparent and unalterable way.

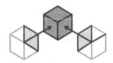

 The transaction is complete

BENEFITS OF THE BLOCKCHAIN

 TRANSPARENCY AND TRACKING

 SIMPLER AND FASTER

 REDUCED COSTS

 INCREASED TRUST

BLOCKCHAIN TECHNOLOGY USES

DIGITAL CURRENCY

IOT

GOVERNANCE

HEALTHCARE

FINANCE

DATA STORAGE

ONLINE VOTING

INSURANCE

DO THIS **ACTION STEPS**

1. Visit **dorethiakelly.com/crypto** to learn the basics in an easy-to-understand way.

 ## SAY THIS **#MONEYCHAT MANTRAS**

“ *I will make educated investing decisions*

“ *I will only do what's right for my financial situation regardless of popular opinion*

CHAPTER 12

Retirement

#MoneyChat

"Many people take no care of their money 'til they come nearly to the end of it, and others do just the same with their time."
—Johann Wolfgang Von Goethe

IN A SURVEY CONDUCTED BY *the Employee Benefit Research Institute,* only 73% of people polled were confident they'd have enough money in retirement.[18] What about you? Do you think you'll have enough?

Do you have dreams about lazy days by the pool or nightmares about living out of a cardboard box?

How Much Will You Need?

Do the math. Can you live on less than your income or will you want it to stay the same? Realistically, most people want to keep the same lifestyle in retirement. If you earn $60,000 now, do you really want to live on $40,000 in retirement? Be honest with yourself and calculate the true amount you'd like to work with each year. For those who may have to care for their parents or their grandchildren, it would be wise to include an estimate of those annual costs as well. As we age, our healthcare costs rise. There may be more doctor visits, prescriptions and, possibly, hospitalizations. It's better to face the possibility than be unprepared when the time comes. But on a more upbeat note—add travel! You've worked hard all your life and you should enjoy yourself, so be sure to throw in some money for travel and other things you love!

Seriously consider how you can get rid of debt using the strategies I've outlined in Sections 1: Getting Out of the Hole and Section 2: Getting on Solid Ground in the years leading up to your retirement. You want to enter retirement with the least amount of debt possible and a sure financial footing.

When Should You Start?

It's ideal to begin saving for retirement from the moment you start your first job, but we all know it doesn't quite work out that way for many of us. Therefore, when you start will depend on your income, expenses, goals, and age.

Here are some rules of thumb you may be able to apply to your situation:

Minimal Debt: Money left each month after bills are paid? The sky's the limit! Contribute the maximum of 15% and take advantage of the full match from your employer. If you aren't quite ready to contribute 15%, start where you can (ideally, at least 6%) and build up over time. Some employers may require you to put in a certain percent before they'll match your savings. If so, put in at least that amount. You can contribute less; you just won't receive the match.

Significant Debt: Press pause on any retirement savings. I'd say don't contribute until you at least pay down some of your smaller debts.

If you're in your 20s and 30s and have a lot of debt, you still have time to focus on getting rid of it over the next few years. You can start saving for retirement once you've become financially stable and still pay off debt. After you've gotten rid of a large chunk of your outstanding debts, you'll be able to contribute more money to your retirement when you do start again.

If you are past the age of 40 and have a large amount of debt, focus on eliminating as much debt as possible over the next two to three years. After that, allocate the money you now have from the paid off debt to saving for retirement and continue to pay off any remaining debt. At this point in your life, you're much closer to retirement and need to begin to take advantage of employer matching and tax-deferred contributions.

Now, the key is to make sure you're not incurring any new debt and have a debt payoff plan. Otherwise, you won't change your situation. Ten years could go by, and you'd still be in the same place financially.

Keep Up With Your Accounts

As you switch jobs, you may forget that you had a pension here or there. (I was guilty of this once.) It's important to know what you'll have coming in during your retirement years. Contact all previous and current employers about your retirement plan with them. Ask for an estimate of your payout at retirement. Be sure to read all the notices you get in the mail about your retirement plan. They often discuss changes or updates to your benefits. Also, contact the Social Security Administration periodically to see what amount you may receive from them. You can move your pensions and retirement accounts to a new employer account or your personal IRAs. Best to speak to a financial advisor about your specific situation.

Only Have an Account With Your Employer?

Please do not only have a retirement account with your employer. Invest in an IRA on your own. None of us could miss the countless news stories about employees who lost everything when their employer's stock hit rock bottom. Many of you probably knew someone personally that this happened to. It's important to use various retirement investing strategies. In the event one account doesn't do so well, you'll still have money elsewhere to soften the blow.

Types of Employer Plans

401(k): This is a very common retirement plan offered by employers. It's a replacement for older pension plans. When you enroll in a 401(k), you can contribute a percentage of your pre-tax earnings into the plan.

The managers of the plan then invest the money into mutual funds to grow it over time. When you reach retirement age, you pay taxes on the money as you withdraw it.

This leads to significant tax savings over your working life. There are also significant tax penalties for withdrawing money early, though in some cases you can get a loan from the money that's been placed in one.

Many companies will match what you put in if you've worked for them for a number of years. So, if you contribute 10% of your pre-tax paycheck, they will put in that same dollar amount, giving you a significant boost to your capital. There are varieties of these plans, such as a 403(b), which is reserved for educators and nonprofits; and a 457, which is offered to government employees.

Roth 401(k): This is a form of 401(k) that combines the advantages of a 401(k) with an IRA. (More on that in a bit.) With a Roth 401(k), your contribution is taken out of your paycheck *after* taxes, but then there are no further taxes on anything earned in the account. The money you withdraw from the account after you retire isn't taxed either.

Thrift Savings Plan (TSP): Thrift Savings Plans are essentially 401(k) plans for military and civilian government employees. Employees contribute pretax dollars from their paychecks and the government agency they work for matches up to a certain percent of their salary. Just as with a 401(k), employees pay taxes upon withdrawing their savings and are penalized if they do so before reaching age 59½. There is also a Roth version of the TSP that allows employees to make after-tax contributions.

457 and 403 (b): These types of accounts are used by nonprofits, public schools, colleges, and state and local governments. They operate much like the 401(k) where employees contribute pre-tax earnings out of their paycheck and taxes are deferred until the money is withdrawn at retirement. Unfortunately, withdrawals during retirement are taxed as regular income on these accounts, but the thought is that, in retirement, you'll be in a lower income tax bracket than when you were working.

There are also differences between these accounts and a 401(k) as it relates to distributions. With the 457 plan, you can withdraw your money without penalties if you leave the job, whether or not you're 59½. With the 403b, there's a 10% penalty for any kind of early withdrawal.

Individual Retirement Plans

Traditional Individual Retirement Arrangement (IR A) : If your employer doesn't offer any of the plans that were just mentioned, you can go to any bank or brokerage firm and open up an individual retirement arrangement.

An IRA is a tax-deferred account. The income in one doesn't have to be reported to the IRS until you withdraw it. After withdrawal, the money is taxed. There's a limit to how much you can put into an IRA every year, but it's high enough that you can build a very nice nest egg. Once the money is in the account, you can invest it however you like into many different types of securities. And just like a 401(k), you can't withdraw the money from the account before retirement age without significant penalties.

ROTH IRA: A Roth IRA takes after-tax dollars and puts them into an IRA account. Because you make contributions after taxes, you don't have to worry about paying more taxes on any money that's added to the account. It's very common to have both a 401(k) and a Roth IRA for a complete investment package. The 401(k) provides long-term benefits while the Roth IRA can be used for emergencies between now and retirement, and still provide a solid retirement nest egg. The contribution limit in a Roth is similar to that of a standard IRA.

SIMPLE IRA: This is a form of 401(k) for small businesses. A company can have no more than 100 employees in order to be eligible for this kind of plan. From an employee point of view, this type of account is very similar to a 401(k). If you're an employer, you'll pay less into the plan than you would a 401(k).

SIMPLIFIED EMPLOYEE PENSION PLAN (SEP IRA): If you're completely self-employed and have no one working for you, then the SEP IRA is the way to go. SEP IRAs are great if the income you're bringing in far exceeds the limit you can put into an IRA. There's no IRS filing requirement for this plans and the paperwork is minimal. However, determining how much you can contribute each year can be a little confusing. If you're going for the maximum contribution, it's around 25% of your net profit.

Whichever of these plans is right for you, it's better to get started earlier rather than later. The more you put in earlier, the larger your investment has a chance to grow over time. Just because your job doesn't offer a 401(k) doesn't mean you can't start saving for retirement now. Talk with your financial advisor for more information about these plans and what you can do to start making contributions right away.

Even if you are not nearing or at retirement age, AARP is one of the best sites to go to for information. Go to **www.aarp.org**. Also, be sure to check out **www.myretirementblog.com/**.

DO THIS ACTION STEP
Do Your Research!

1. **Check whether your company picks up the tab.**

   There are administrative expenses associated with running the plan that your employer is responsible for. In large companies, this expense is not passed on to the employees. However, in some smaller companies it is. Ask your plan sponsor if you are responsible for this expense.

2. **Review your investment expenses.**

   a. Secure a copy of your most recent investment statement. If you're not currently enrolled in your plan, you can either perform this review on all the funds available in your plan or preselect funds you are interested in.

b.   Look for the expense ratio for each fund you want to analyze. You can find this information on your 401(k) website or in the fund prospectus. Expense ratios are expressed as an annual percentage of your total investments.

c.   Calculate and find the total annual cost of each investment by multiplying the fund's expense ratio by your ending balance. For example, if you have $3,000 in an investment and its expense ratio is 0.20%, then you're paying $6 a year. You want to shoot for a total expense ratio between 1-1.5%.

3.   Make a decision.

Once you've discovered your final cost and compared it to comparable plans, you can make an educated decision about how much to invest in your retirement for each paycheck.

 SAY THIS **#MONEYCHAT MANTRAS**

" *I will retire wealthy*

" *Retirement will be some of my best years*

CHAPTER 13

Retirement Investing for Young Adults with Manyell Akinfe-Reed

#MoneyChat

"Don't simply retire from something; have something to retire to."
—Harry Emerson Fosdick

THE ECONOMIC LANDSCAPE FOR YOUNG adults today is a lot different than it was for the generation before them. Not long ago, achieving the American Dream was a sure shot. You worked for 30 years; invested in a defined contribution plan, such as a 401(k) or 403(b); put money aside for a rainy day and retired with a hefty pension. Without a doubt you'd be able to buy a home and send your kids to school. Everything would inevitably work out if you just worked hard. Unfortunately, the terrain for Generations X, Y and Z has been rockier. They've seen unemployment skyrocket, financial markets explode, education costs soar, a housing market crash and pensions vanish. On top of all that, they have also experienced a pandemic, something none of us expected! While we'll never be able to control the market, young adults can stack the odds in their favor by avoiding common mistakes when preparing for their future.

Avoid Wasting Time

Time is the most powerful asset young adults have when preparing for retirement, yet only 56% of workers ages 25–34, and 63% of workers ages 35–44, say they've begun saving.[19] For most of us, just thinking about saving enough is daunting. According to the retirement calculators I've used, I'll need $1.8 million to retire comfortably by age 67. Looking at all my current responsibilities and thinking of future ones, this number would drive me mad if I didn't understand that putting time on my side increases the number of years my money will grow and decreases the monthly amount I need to set aside.

Let's look at it in action. If you had a choice between receiving $100,000 toward your retirement today or a penny that doubled for 30 years, which would you choose? Most would choose the $100,000 and miss out on a whopping $10.7 million.

Grow, Penny, Grow

YEARS	INTEREST EARNED	YOUR BALANCE
1	$0.01	$0.02
2	$0.02	$0.04
3	$0.04	$0.08
4	$0.08	$0.16
5	$0.16	$0.32
10	$5.12	$10.24
15	$163.84	$327.68
20	$5,242.88	$10,485.76
25	$167,772.16	$335,544.32
30	$5,368,708.80	$10,737,417.00

Although financial institutes don't offer an annual percentage rate of 100%, the above example illustrates the power of compound interest. Compound interest is the concept of earning interest on top of interest. It's the reason a penny can grow to $10 million dollars without another cent being added to the account. Each year, the dollar amount of interest earned increases in response to a growing balance. Without compounding, the account would have only gained $0.01 a year and grown to a measly

$0.30. You can apply this same concept to a more realistic example and get the same shocking results. A 25-year-old contributing $100 a month to a retirement account until age 67 and receiving an annual 6% in interest will amass $212,296! And 6% is a very conservative return. For a 25-year-old whose portfolio is properly allocated to include more exposure to stocks, we can expect to see an 8% return. Using the same monthly contribution and retirement age, the account would grow to $367,626.

Getting a head start saving will also lower your monthly retirement bill, making it easier to fit into your budget. Let's say the same 25-year-old above, earning the 8%, discovered they would need $800,000 to retire comfortably. To achieve this goal, they would need to save $285[20] dollars a month. If this same person delays saving until age 35, they would need to save $588[21] per month. That additional $303 a month could be used to pay off debt, save for college or take a vacation. What the money is used for is insignificant compared to the high price that's paid for procrastinating.

 DO THIS **ACTION STEPS**
Level Set!

1. Don' t freak out.

   It's easy to get paralysis of analysis and dwell on how much you'll need. Accept that it's a big number and start working on a plan.

2. Fast forward.

   The amount you'll need in retirement will depend on several variables, such as the age you start saving, when you want to retire, your life expectancy, how much you plan to withdraw annually and much more. Before determining how much you need, you'll have to spend some time thinking about what you want your golden years to look like.

3.   Determine how much you'll need in retirement.

Less than half of all workers have tried to calculate how much they're going to need to save for retirement.[22] There's no way to develop an effective strategy if you don't know what you're aiming for. The Internet offers a wide selection of retirement calculators for free. When deciding which calculator to use, select the one that allows for the highest number of variables you could think of in the Fast Forward exercise above. The calculator should also give explanations for each field available so that you're clear on the assumptions used to calculate the recommended amount. I like the Ultimate Retirement Calculator on millionaire and financial coach Todd Tresidder's website. It's available for free.

Take the Money on the Table

Young adults are leaving far too much money on the table. If your employer matches contributions made to their retirement plan, you should at least be making the minimum contribution to receive the match—PERIOD! The one caveat is that you pay very close attention to the fees you're being charged in your plan. If your plan is too expensive, it may be in your best interest to consider an alternate investment vehicle.

The Department of Labor's Employee Benefits Security Administration has a rule that requires employers to provide fee disclosures to participants in 401(k)-type plans. The information provided must include what was actually charged or deducted from your account, along with a description of what the charge was for. Previously, this information was not available, and many employees had no idea how much it was costing them to participate in their employer retirement plan. According to a survey conducted by AARP, 71% of respondents didn't even know they were paying fees.[23] Having this information not only gives us the opportunity to decide if we're paying too much, but it also enables us to consider these expenses in our retirement planning.

The fees and expenses in your plan will fall into two categories: administrative and investment. Administrative fees pay for your being a part of the plan and investment fees are associated with your individual investment choices.

Administrative charges cover the day-to-day operation of the plan, such as record keeping and customer service. This charge can be picked up by your company, covered by your investment fee or charged directly to the plan. When charged directly to the plan, the expense will get passed on to you as a flat fee or divided between all plan participants in proportion to their account balance. When passed on to plan participants, individuals with higher balances pay a higher percentage of the expense.

Investment fees, the larger of the two expenses, pay for the cost of managing the investments in the plan. These fees are deducted from your investment returns and depend on the type of investments you select, as well as the company providing the service. When reviewing your investment choices, you want to pick options with the lowest expenses. As a general rule of thumb, you should aim to pay no more than 1% in administrative fees and less than 1.5% for any given investment in your plan.

A half of a percentage may not seem like a lot of money, but over time it can significantly reduce your account balance as seen below.

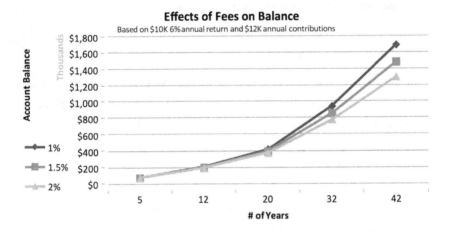

You can't guarantee performance, but you can guarantee that you won't pay high fees.

The Four Stages of Retirement Planning

Allocate Appropriately

Proper asset allocation is essential to reaching your retirement goals. Although there is no one-size-fits-all formula, as a young investor, your time horizon should always be tightly knit to your risk tolerance. Your time horizon is the number of years you have to invest, and your risk tolerance is your willingness and ability to handle fluctuations in the stock and bond markets. A basic investment strategy is to take more risk when you have a long time horizon, and less risk when you don't. With the number of years your money will need to last increasing with life expectancy, the age-old goal of $1M is likely not enough. By using the four stages of retirement planning outlined below as a guide, you can rest assured that you've done your part in setting your portfolio up for optimal growth.

Stage 1: Accumulation

The accumulation stage starts as soon as you have a job. If you're under 21, you probably won't be able to invest in your employer's plan. But any investor with earned income can open an Individual Retirement Account (IRA). In this first stage of your retirement planning, amassing wealth is your primary objective. Therefore, I recommend a portfolio of 85–100% stocks. By investing in stocks, you expose your portfolio to more risk in exchange for a higher return. This level of exposure will surely have its ups and downs, but understanding historical performance will help you stay the course.

The S&P 500 is the most commonly used benchmark for the U.S. stock market. Over the past 32 years, it has averaged a return of 11.2%. Calculated in this return are the major dips the stock market took that both Generation X and Y experienced, including its -37% return in 2008. The Barclays Capital Aggregated Bond Index, which is the benchmark for bonds, returned only 8.5% over the same period. That's a 2.7% difference! You'll need the high returns of the stock market to lay the foundation for your savings, and this is the only stage where you can take high risks because of the time you'll have to recover from losses.

Stage 2: Preservation

The preservation stage starts nine to 10 years before you retire. During this stage, your focus is on protecting your money. The old school of investing would suggest reducing your stock exposure to below 50%. I strongly suggest a 50/50 split between stocks and bonds. During this stage, I recommend hiring a fee-only advisor to go over your retirement goals and discuss with you whether you should scale back further from stocks. Your advisor will be able to give you a deeper understanding of the direction of the markets. Nearly one in four investors ages 56 to 65 had more than 90% percent of their account balances in stocks going into 2008, according to the Employee Benefit Research Institute. I don't know what age these individuals planned to retire, but I can guarantee you their timelines have been altered due to the effects the downturn had on their portfolio. No one can guarantee returns but a good financial advisor can make you aware of trends in the market that you should avoid or take advantage of.

Stage 3: Distribution

This is the stage in which you have retired, and your objective is to ensure that your money is outpacing inflation. Let's assume an inflation rate between 2.5% to 3%. During this time, you should have 75%–85% of your money invested in bonds. Don't risk your savings, regardless of how well the market is performing, unless you are okay with the possibility of running out of money. There will be little to no time for recovering from a major downturn in the economy.

Stage 4: Transfer

The final stage, which is too often forgotten, is the transfer stage. Who do you want to reap the benefits of your hard work? Be sure that the beneficiaries on all your accounts are up to date. Retirement assets pass directly to beneficiaries without having to go through the long and costly process of probate court. Although your beneficiaries will avoid probate, they still may be responsible for federal and state income taxes on the money they receive. Inform your beneficiaries of this and provide them with a copy of any forms that name them as such. Make them aware that there may be tax liabilities associated with their payout, so they're not caught by surprise.

 DO THIS ACTION STEPS
What is Your Risk Tolerance?

1. Assess your risk tolerance.

    There is a slew of risk tolerance surveys on the Internet. A Google search returned 1,650M results, so you won't have trouble finding a few to take. Even if you think you know your risk tolerance and have been investing for some time, it's good to take part in this exercise. It may reveal information that was hidden before.

2. Choose a direction.

    The purpose of risk tolerance questionnaires is to give you direction. They're not intended to be a one-stop shop for asset allocation. You will ultimately tailor your final allocations based on things no questionnaire can address, such as your fear of losing money because your mom lost her savings when the dotcom bubble burst, or your love of bonds because you saw your grandma play it safe and win. In this step, you'll need to consider how much money you have to risk, what risk you're required to take to meet your goals and the effects different levels of risk have on your portfolio.

    If you're already saving for retirement, you can use portfolio analysis software on sites like PersonalCapital.com and Morningstar. com to see if your current asset allocation is where you want it. If it's not, you can adjust your percentages in each fund until they are aligned with where you want them going forward. Both sites provide commentary that can be used to guide your decisions.

For new investors, making a decision will require a little more leg work. I suggest selecting a Target-Date Fund from either your employer's retirement plan or a company like Fidelity or Vanguard and inputting the fund's information into the sites I mentioned for portfolio analysis. Target-Date Funds are a mixture of different funds that are allocated based on the date you want to retire. As you get closer to retirement, your stock exposure decreases. Using Target-Date Funds as a guide will help you determine how similar or different you need your asset allocation to be.

3. Take action.

After you've spent time exploring risk and determining the approach you want to take, it's time to take action. If you're still unsure, ask for help. Every financial company that offers products has customer service representatives that can answer questions about the investments they provide. They won't be able to give you financial advice, but they can give you general information on the investment and its performance. Some employers provide access to financial advisors free of charge. Check with your employer to see if this is available to you.

Final Thoughts

Putting time on your side, taking advantage of your employer's match and having the proper asset allocation is just the beginning of your investing journey. Throughout your trip you will need to remain positive, perform regular checkups and maintain a long term perspective. For the majority of us saving for retirement is the largest financial goal we will have to accomplish. You can borrow money for college or to buy a house but here are no loans for retirement. Social security will offer some assistance, but proper planning will always be the cornerstone of a long term investment strategy. With the cost of living increases, staggering health care cost and a troubled social security system we must be proactive in planning our financial future to accumulate an adequate retirement fund.

1. Maintain a positive attitude.

   Don't look at saving as a burden. Focus on how you'll feel once you've reached your goal and take pride in knowing you're taking steps to plan your tomorrow today.

2. Perform checkups.

   Examine your progress at least twice a year. Make sure you're on track to retire at your desired age. Confirm that your money will last throughout retirement and that you'll be able to afford the lifestyle you want during retirement. Here is where the Ultimate Retirement Calculator I mentioned previously can help.

3. Keep a long-term perspective.

   Sometimes you'll look at your balance and feel like you'll never reach your goal. You'll come up with a million and one reasons to withdraw your money. Don't do it! Remember—you can only replace lost time with more money, and who's signing up for that?

FINANCIAL EXPERT MANYELL AKINFE-REED has been a Reuters, CNBC and Black Enterprise Business Report contributor and an active volunteer for several community programs increasing the financial literacy of New Yorkers.

CHAPTER 14

The Truth About Saving for College

#MoneyChat

"Education is our passport to the future, for tomorrow belongs to the people who prepare for it today."
—Malcom X

The Value of Vocational School

Want to earn 6 figures without a 6 figure student loan bill? Then don't discount vocational school. There are a lot of successful careers developed in trade schools that. I'm very well paper trained, I have degrees, so I am pro college. I'm also pro vocational school because I know college isn't for everyone, we need people to take advantage of BOTH career paths as economically as possible.

Grab your list of career paths that pay well, without the big college bill at **dorethiakelly.com/moneychathub**

What College Will Likely Cost in Five, 10, 20 Years

According to the Education Data Initiative, college tuition inflation averaged 4.63% each year from 2010 to 2020. [24,25] Historically, college tuition prices double every 10 to 12 years and, from the looks of things, that's not about to change. The cost of higher education is going to get, well, *higher*! In fact, the U.S. Department of Education estimates that the average cost of a four-year education will be $203,000 by the year 2030.

On average, you can expect college expenses to increase between 5% and 7% each year. Knowing that, you can estimate what college will likely cost when your child graduates from high school, whether that's in five years or 17 years. There's a quick and easy calculator on finaid.org that you can use to determine how much money you'll need to save for college. When you calculate, be sure to include all costs—not only tuition, but also room and board, books, and other expenses. Then start saving as soon as you can, the earlier the better. A 529 Savings Plan and a Coverdell ESA are two tax-advantaged investment accounts we'll talk about that you'll want to look into.

Why Does It Cost So Much?

Colleges receive money from a variety of sources:

- Tuition and fees

- Federal, state and local (city) funds

- Endowment income (money or property donated to an institution)

Schools need this money to cover their expenses, which include hiring quality professors, making improvements to the facility and so on. Over time, buildings age, technology changes and expenses rise. This means income sources must keep pace. How schools do this appears to differ between public and private institutions, however. According to the Delta Cost Project, both types of colleges rely on tuition and fees but "increases in tuition and fees were the single largest source of revenue for private institutions, while state and local appropriations remain the largest revenue category for public institutions." (Source: The Growing Imbalance, http://**www.deltacostproject.org**) This is a good reason to take a long, hard look at the cost differences between a public and private education.

Make a Plan. And Stick to It.

Whether your children are toddlers or teenagers, it's never too late or too early to start saving for college. Of course, the amount you can save will be based on your budget and household expenses. But it's important to set a goal, even if you'll have to begin later. Don't allow the costs of college to overwhelm you. Do what you can. Create a strategy for where you are now and stick to it.

Do the math

1. How long do you have before your child/children graduate high school?

2. How much can you afford to set aside each month?

Let's say the average cost of college, whether private or public, is $25,000 per year. Remember that this amount fluctuates depending on the school. It also doesn't take into consideration inflation or annual tuition increases, but it's a good starting point. So, let's crunch the numbers.

Average annual cost of college:

$25,000 x 4 years = $100,000

Number of years until your child graduates = 7

$100,000/7 years = $14,285 per year

$14,285/12 mos. = $1,190 = the amount you would need to save each month for the next seven years

Whoa! That's a lot of money, right? Okay, don't panic.

Of course, the younger your children are, the more time you have to save. So, if you have a newborn to elementary student and have disposable income, you're in great shape. But let's suppose you can't put away the amount suggested in our example above. The average family can't put $1,200 toward college savings each month. In fact, many families already have children in high school already and haven't been able to save much at all. Don't get discouraged. Look at your personal finances and decide on a reasonable amount you can invest each month. Now develop a plan each year to increase that amount. Based on our example, the college-bound child is in the sixth grade (because the parent(s) have seven years to save). Here's the plan the child's parent(s) developed to set aside college funds. (This is a basic college savings plan. It doesn't take into consideration the interest that will accrue and increase the funds available.)

# OF YEARS	MONTHLY SAVINGS	ANNUAL SAVINGS	TOTAL
YEAR 1	150	1,800	1,800
YEAR 2	200	2,400	4,200
YEAR 3	250	3,000	7,200
YEAR 4	300	3,600	10,800
YEAR 5	300	3,600	14,400
YEAR 6	350	4,200	18,600
YEAR 7	350	4,200	**22,800**

As you can see, this child's parent(s) will end up with $22,800 when the child is graduating high school! Now, that may not cover all four years, but it will definitely cover one year. And depending on the school, it may even cover two years.

Another thing to consider is that you can continue to sock away money while your child is in college for the next three years. Whether you're able to save more or less each year, it's important to develop a plan for the time you have. Being able to get an idea of how the savings will add up over the years allows parents to research additional resources—such as scholarships, dual enrollment, work study, etc.—to make up the difference.

Do Your Homework

Begin researching schools, criteria for qualifying for scholarships and other potential tuition-reducing programs. For example, students who serve as resident assistants in their dorms during their junior and senior years won't have to pay for room and board those two years.

In planning for your children's college education, keep one thing in mind: Generally, no one pays the sticker price, that is, the actual, quoted cost of attending a particular school before grants and other financial aid is applied. Regardless of your income, you probably won't either. If you find that the costs are more than you want to pay, community college is an excellent option for your child's first two years of college.

Deciding Where to Put It

You've decided to invest for your children's education—kudos to you! Now where to save may be a slightly tougher decision. We're here to help! Below are four college savings investing options for you to evaluate. Consider which one—or which combination—is best for your family.

529 College Savings Plans

529 College Savings Plans are a very attractive solution for saving for college. They were created in 1996 in Section 529 of the IRS code—hence its name. They are essentially mutual funds for college savings, so

they contain a mix of investments in stocks, bonds, real estate and money market funds. Over the life of the account, contribution limits range from $100,000–$300,000, based on the rules of your state, and your money grows tax-free. And you're not limited to investing in a 529 Plan in the state you live in. If another state offers the best plan for your goals, you can invest there. Another good thing about 529 Plans are their low investment minimums. In most cases, you can open an account with as little as $25. There's also no age limit on beneficiaries or time limit on distributions.

Eligibility: There are no limitations on eligibility for a 529 Plan. Anyone can open an account.

Taxes: You won't pay any federal taxes if the money is used for qualified school expenses: tuition, books, fees, room and board. Normally, you wouldn't pay any state taxes either, but each state sets its own rules. You can't deduct 529 Plan contributions on your federal income taxes, but some states allow a tax deduction.

While you may be able to contribute large amounts in one year— be careful. You could incur a gift tax if you go over the maximum gift allowance of 13,000 per year. Stay below this annual maximum to make sure you avoid this tax.

Returns: A Word to the Wise

Pay attention to the investments in the 529 Plan you choose. There are various options based on the age of your student and your risk tolerance. Remember to research the investments contained in the plans. Do they have solid returns of 8%–10% or more over a 10-year period? If not, you may want to choose another state's plan. Financial advisors and their clients are noticing that some 529 Plans aren't performing as well as expected. They're getting the same return you would get from simply having your money in a savings account! Ouch!

Coverdell Education Savings Accounts (ESAs)

Coverdell ESAs, also known as Education IRAs, are another option for saving for college that also invests in stocks, CDs, mutual funds, bonds and money market funds. You can only contribute $2,000 per year, but that's a great starting point for many families until they are able to contribute more. Since you contribute after-tax earnings, the money is withdrawn tax-free when your child is ready for college. The beneficiary must be under 18 when the account is opened and the money has to be used by the child's thirtieth birthday.

There are limitations on who can contribute to a Coverdell ESA:

- If you're single, your annual income must be under $95,000.

- If you're married, your annual income must be under $190,000.

Other State-Sponsored Savings Plans

Many states offer savings plans that help you save for your child's college now. Basically, these programs allow you to pre-pay a part of your child's tuition before he or she is ready to go to college. This gives the child a huge head start and makes it much easier to budget out the costs of college over time. A prime example of a state-sponsored savings plan is the Michigan Education Trust (michigan. gov/setwithmet). Others can be found via the College Savings Plans Network website (collegesavings.org).

One caveat is that the money in many state-sponsored savings programs must be used for public, in-state schools. Some programs may offer a refund that allows you to apply the money to other schools, but it may not be the same amount as if your child stayed in state. Further, the money saved in these programs can only go toward tuition. It doesn't cover other college-related expenses, such as room and board, and books. You can, however, transfer the funds to siblings or first cousins if, for some reason, the original recipient chooses not attend college.

Mutual Funds

Mutual funds are not the best types of investment for your child's education because you'll be taxed on the capital gains you earn each year. It can work if you have a fund that's outperforming each year, thus offsetting the taxes you'd have to pay. But I'm not so sure it's worth the hassle when you have other college savings options. Also, the contributions you make to a mutual fund aren't tax deductible. If anything, mutual funds as a college savings vehicle should be a last resort.

What about using a 401(k) or other retirement accounts?

Your children will have many options for paying for college when the time comes. You, on the other hand, will not when it comes to your retirement. And nine times out of 10, your children will not be in a position to help you. Guard your retirement savings like a hawk and keep it intact. Definitely do not raid it to pay for college expenses. The key is to definitely have a college savings strategy. Don't feel like a bad parent if you can't pay 100% of your child's tuition, especially if you have more than one child. Again, there are several options for paying for college. You don't have to deplete your personal or retirement savings.

DO THIS ACTION STEPS
Offset the Rising Cost of College!

Here are a few things you can begin doing now to offset the rising cost of college:

1. **Calculate.** Use this calculator at savingforcollege.com to determine what college will cost by the time your children are ready to attend.

2. **Budget.** Look at your household budget and determine how much you can begin to save for each of your children. Contact your financial advisor to determine what type of college savings investment plan is best for you.

3. **Tutoring.** Prepare your children academically—via tutoring, enrichment programs, etc.—so they'll do well in class and on college entrance exams. This will make them attractive candidates for scholarships and grants when they apply to colleges. Tip: start now making sure they write excellent essays; this is one thing that we look for when judging scholarships. If the essay has grammar mistakes, poor writing, they are dismissed within the first few sentences. Make sure your student is READING, has a good vocabulary, excellent grammar and can WRITE.

4. **Guide your children.** What's most important is that your kids become responsible adults who contribute good to society and can earn money to take care of themselves. Don't assume college is for them. Guide and direct, but don't count out community college and vocational schools. **There are a lot of people with a vocational education earning more than college students without the expense. As I said before,** I'm not knocking college, my point is there is room for every path—except the **'do nothing'** one. That is not an option!

SAY THIS #MONEYCHAT MANTRAS

" *For your own education:*

" *I will read the fine print*

" *I will seek out scholarships to further my education*

" *I will develop a plan to pay back my student loans*

" *I will not feel guilty for taking out student loans*

 ## FOR YOUR KIDS' EDUCATION

" *I will ensure my children apply for scholarships*

" *I will not feel guilty for not paying for my children's college education I will start saving as soon as I'm able for my kid's education*

SECTION FOUR

SECURING YOUR MONEY

CHAPTER 15

Insurance Simplified

#MoneyChat

"Your peace of mind is worth more than a dime any day."
—Dorethia Kelly

Life Insurance

"Do I *really need* life insurance?" is a question I often get from the #MONEYCHAT fam, and my answer is always yes. I'm sure you've heard a few stories of people struggling to make ends meet after their loved one passes. Taking out a life insurance policy can ensure that your loved ones aren't left with a financial burden while also mourning. No one likes to talk about death, but death is the only thing in life that's guaranteed so we must prepare for it.

What is Life Insurance?

Life insurance is an insurance policy that pays out a lump sum to your beneficiaries when you die. The payout is called a death benefit and the best part is this: It's not taxed as income! Once life insurance is in place, you can sit back and relax. Insurance coverage can last for several years, or even decades, as long as you don't let the coverage lapse.

What Can Life Insurance Cover?

Paying for burial and funeral costs isn't the only thing life insurance can do. The payout can give loved ones the money they need to settle your affairs and establish a new financial normal without you. These are key things life insurance can do:

- **Settle your debts:** The payout can clear debt you carry, such as student loans, a mortgage, or a car loan, as instructed in your will.

- **Bridge the gap:** A life insurance policy can cover the financial gap that your family may face when they can no longer rely on your income. It's an additional source of money on top of your 401k or Roth IRA that they can pull from until they get back on their feet.

- **Build generational wealth:** A life insurance policy is one of the best ways to pass along wealth. Insurance companies may offer policies that pay several times your annual salary. Think about what a six-figure life insurance payout could do for your husband, wife, son, or daughter. Maybe it could send your child to college, or it could be used as a down payment on an investment property. The options are endless!

Types of Life Insurance Policies

Under the umbrella term "life insurance" there are two main categories—term life insurance and permanent life insurance.

Term Life Insurance

Term life insurance covers you for a specific time period and only offers a death benefit. Once the coverage period of your term life insurance policy ends, your death is no longer covered. I recommend starting with term life insurance because it's straightforward and usually cheap.

Permanent Insurance

Permanent life insurance is—you guessed it—a policy that you have permanently as long as you pay the premiums. On top of the death benefit, a permanent life insurance policy typically comes with a savings or investment account that you can tap into while you're still alive.

The money you sock away in the account is called your "cash value." Tax on the account is deferred, which means you don't have to pay taxes on the gains—Score! There are several types of permanent policies that come with different (and sometimes confusing) contract terms. Here's a breakdown of common types and how they work:

- **Traditional whole life insurance:** A permanent life insurance policy that has a death benefit and part of your premium goes into a savings account that you may be able to withdraw or borrow from while you're alive.

- **Final expense (or burial) insurance:** A smaller whole life insurance policy that's meant to only pay for the cost of death and burial.

- **Universal life insurance:** A permanent life insurance policy that has a death benefit and savings account, but you have a bit more flexibility. You may be able to change your premium payment and your death benefit without getting a new policy once you've built up enough cash value.

- **Variable life insurance:** A permanent life insurance policy that comes with a death benefit and an investment account instead of a savings account. With an investment account there's an opportunity for your money to grow exponentially, but there's also a risk that your account could lose value.

- **Variable universal life insurance:** A permanent life insurance policy with a death benefit and the investment component, but you may have more investment control and the option to make policy changes.

BENEFICIARIES

If you are single, use your parents, responsible adult children, or trusted siblings for beneficiaries and not your boyfriend or girlfriend.

How Much Does Life Insurance Cost?

The cost can vary depending on your lifestyle, health, and how old you are. In fact, you may be able to get life insurance for around the same price as renter's insurance—or even cheaper.

According to a ValuePenguin 2020 insurance quote study, a 20-year term life insurance policy with a $500,000 death benefit costs just $25.67 to $38.14 per month on average for non-smokers between the ages of 25 and 40.

Permanent life insurance policies tend to be more expensive than term life insurance policies. A simple and affordable term life insurance policy may be all you need for now as long as it covers your final expenses and settles your affairs.

How to Get Life Insurance

Your employer could have a group life insurance policy that covers employees, but that may or may not be enough. The steps for getting your own policy are pretty painless.

First, you need to figure out how much coverage you need. If you work with a financial advisor, they can make a recommendation. If you're shopping for coverage alone, try using an online insurance calculator at Bankrate.com or Policygenius.com to figure out how much you need.

Next, get three to five quotes from a licensed insurance provider. During the application, insurance companies will ask questions about your health, and they'll use the information to decide whether to cover you and at what premium.

What if you have preexisting conditions?

As harsh as it sounds, the life insurance business is…well, a business. It's truly sad, but being of a certain age or having health conditions can make it hard to get affordable coverage. Guaranteed issue and simplified issue life insurance are two unique policies to consider if you're unable to get another policy.

Simplified issue life insurance is a life insurance policy that you can get quickly with just a few health questions and no medical exam.

Guaranteed issue life insurance is a life insurance policy that you can get without answering *any* questions about your health. Age and coverage restrictions may apply. For example, Fidelity Life has a guaranteed whole life policy for adults between the ages of 50 to 85 that has a death benefit of up to $25,000.

Other Insurance Policies to Consider

Aging, getting sick, or getting injured is also expensive and important to prepare for as well. Disability insurance can replace part of your income if you're unable to work because of an accident or debilitating illness. Short-term or long-term disability insurance may be offered by your employer. Long-term care insurance policies can pay for care that's not covered by Medicare or health insurance, such as the cost of a home nurse or health aid.

STORING YOUR DOCUMENTS

Your life insurance policy is one of those important documents that you need to keep somewhere safe. Think about investing in a safe or locked filing cabinet. If you prefer going paperless, you can store files digitally on a secure cloud drive or external hard drive—the keyword being SECURE.

Insurance Terms Explained

While shopping for coverage, these are some common terms you may see and what they mean:

- **Beneficiary:** The person or persons who you assign to receive the lump sum from your life insurance payout.

- **Living benefit:** A rider that may be added to an insurance policy that provides benefits while you're still alive like an advanced payout.

- **Premiums:** The amount you pay for the insurance policy.

- **Power of attorney:** A person that you give permission to act on your behalf. In the case of life insurance, this could be the person that you allow to make payments or policy changes if you're unable to do so on your own.

- **Rider:** An amendment to contract terms that makes a change to your policy.

- **Underwriter:** The person who reviews your application to decide whether to insure you and for what premium.

Well, will you look at that? We've talked about death and life insurance, and it wasn't that bad! Before I close this chapter, I want to leave you with a few final thoughts: Don't wait until it's too late to make sure you and your family are covered. And YES, even young people need life insurance.

INSURANCE CHEAT SHEET

- **What is life insurance?**

  - Life insurance pays out a lump sum to your beneficiaries when you die; the payout is called a death benefit.

- **What can life insurance do?**

  - Pay for funeral and burial expenses.

  - Pay off your outstanding debt.

  - Be a source of income for family members.

  - Pass on generational wealth to your beneficiaries.

- **What are the types of insurance policies?**

  - **Term** life insurance: Covers a specific term and has a death benefit.

  - **Permanent insurance:** Covers you permanently with a death benefit and cash value. These are the types of permanent policies we discussed in this chapter:

    - **Final expense (or burial) insurance**

    - **Traditional whole life insurance**

    - **Universal life insurance**

    - **Variable life insurance**

    - **Variable universal life insurance**

- **How much does life insurance cost?**

  - The cost can vary; term life insurance may cost as little as $20 to $30 per month.

  - Term life insurance is usually cheaper than permanent life insurance.

- **How can I get life insurance?**

  - Your employer may offer a group life insurance plan, but it may not be enough.

  - Figure out how much coverage you need based on your income and family size.

  - Get three to five quotes from licensed insurance agents.

  - Have the health exams required by the insurance company.

  - Sign your insurance documents.

- **Can I get coverage with preexisting conditions?**

  - Yes—but it may cost more. Guaranteed issue and simplified issue life insurance policies are two options that don't require a full health exam.

- **What other insurance options do I have?**

  - While you're still alive, disability insurance can provide income if you're not able to work. Long-term care insurance may cover health aid costs if you can't take care of yourself.

At the bare minimum, please get a policy that will cover your burial expenses. Please do not leave your loved ones to mourn and have to figure out how to pay for your funeral on top of that. Place the payments on automatic so you never have to worry about it lapsing.

DO THIS ACTION STEPS
How to Secure Your Future With Life Insurance

1. **Figure out how much coverage you need.** You can do this by speaking with a financial advisor or using an online insurance calculator. At a minimum, get $10,000–$20,000 to cover burial costs.

2. **Shop for quotes.** Get at least three to five life insurance quotes within the next week so you can secure a policy within 30 days for you and your immediate family.

3. **Make room in your budget.** If the plan you need is a bit more expensive than you want to pay, *make a way*. Think about it like this: It will be much more expensive for your loved ones if you DON'T have adequate life insurance.

4. **Talk to the family.** Have a conversation with your parents, siblings, and loved ones about their life insurance needs because they need coverage, too. It's important that we educate and help our families in a loving way.

5. **When in doubt, go with term life insurance.** If you are just getting started, go with a simple term life insurance policy no matter what the insurance agent says. It's cheaper and it's simple. You can play with permanent life policies that you can save in and withdraw from later—and that's only if it makes sense.

SAY THIS #MONEYCHAT MANTRAS

" *I will always maintain life insurance coverage*

" *I will educate my circle on the necessity of life insurance*

CHAPTER 16

What You May Not Know About Wills, Trusts, and POA'S (Don't Skip This)

"A lot of people think they don't need a will because they don't have any assets. A will is about more than your net worth."
—Attorney Richelle Lester

IF YOU STILL HAVE "WRITE A WILL" on your to-do list, you're not alone. A 2020 Caring.com survey found that less than one-third of Americans have a will or estate plan. And 30% of people say they don't have one because they don't believe they have enough assets to leave behind.

It's a common misconception that only people with a ton of money in the bank need a will. In reality, often people who assume they don't need a will end up being the ones who need it the most, **according to Richelle Lester, an estate attorney based in Michigan.**

The Importance of a Will

A will is a legal document that explains where your assets should go and who will take care of your dependents (e.g., children and pets) when you pass away.

A will isn't only about distributing money or real estate, says Lester, you can use a will to say who gets family heirlooms, jewelry, electronics, memorabilia, and other items of value. You can also say in your will whether you want to be cremated or buried.

A will names an executor; this is the person who will handle your affairs, such as paying your final bills, distributing money, and making sure the will is executed according to your wishes. The will also names your beneficiaries and contingent beneficiaries; these are the people who will receive your assets and backup beneficiaries if the primary ones pass away.

IMPORTANT

Make sure to update the beneficiaries on your financial accounts because beneficiaries on those accounts can supersede what you put down on your will.

Who Needs a Will?

Everyone—and yes, that even means young people with no kids, property, and very little money in savings! "If something happens to you, it's possible that you could end up with some funds available," said Lester. You could get one last paycheck, an insurance refund, or even a lump sum from a wrongful death settlement. If you don't have a will, the court decides what happens to your affairs, and you don't want a judge deciding how to manage your money.

In the best-case scenario, the court could find an amicable way to distribute your money among loved ones. In the worst-case scenario, family members could be in probate court for several months or years fighting over assets. Or an irresponsible child or cousin could even end up inheriting your estate if they're the next person in line under state law, said Lester. Trust me, you don't want this to happen!

How to Draft a Will

Putting together a basic will isn't difficult and doesn't have to be expensive. First, you need to list out your assets, choose an executor, and decide who will get what.

Then, you can use a template from an online service, such as LegalZoom, to draft a basic will document for less than $100. A more in-depth estate plan from an online service may cost closer to $200. Be careful, though—online services give you a generalized template that you must make sure complies with your state's laws.

An estate attorney is recommended for a personalized will. Sometimes estate attorneys offer free consultations and inexpensive estate planning workshops. If all you need is a will, it could cost anywhere from $150 to $250 to have it drafted by a professional. Full estate plans with estate tax advising and other legal counsel may cost closer to $500, but this could be well worth the investment if you have a more complex financial situation with several assets to pass on.

What Happens When You Pass Away?

The executor files the will with the probate court. Probate court authenticates the will, which is a fancy way of saying that the court determines whether or not it's valid. A will is only valid if it's determined you wrote it while you were in sound mind, and it was signed in the presence of witnesses.

What happens during the probate process can differ from state to state. Generally speaking, the probate court makes sure that bills are paid and waits for a period of time to allow for creditors to claim their part of your estate. The rest of your assets are distributed in the way that you outline in the will. The case may go through probate quickly or it could take years depending on your assets, debts, and if there are any disputes with creditors or between family members.

Trusts—What They Are and Who They Are For

You may have heard the word "trust" before. How does a trust fit into this picture?

A trust is similar to a will in that it's a method used to pass on assets, but it does so in a different way. Establishing a trust puts your assets under a separate legal entity that's managed by a trustee that you appoint.

Once a trust is developed, **you fund the trust** by putting property, savings, investments, or other assets into the name of the trust. From there, the trustee manages the real estate or the money in the trust for the benefit of the beneficiaries while you're alive and after you pass away. The rules of the trust can vary depending on the type of trust you set up.

Here are three key advantages of a trust:

- **It doesn't have to go through court:** Unlike a will, trusts don't have to go through probate court. Instead, the trustee makes sure that funds and property are distributed to your beneficiaries as instructed.

- **It may have tax perks:** Forming a trust could help lower your estate tax. An estate tax is an amount your beneficiary may have to pay on the inheritance.

- **It gives you more control:** You get a say on how the trust can be used and when your beneficiaries will get access to it. For example, you can choose what age your children get the money, so they don't spend it all in one place. You can even specify how they can use the money.

Despite these benefits, a trust is not always necessary and oftentimes a will is sufficient, especially if you need to put a plan in place quickly. A trust is a bit more complicated to establish and can cost over $1,500 to set up.

Trusts often make the most sense for people passing down assets to minor children and those who have property or bank accounts in multiple states, according to Lester. That's because you can be creative with conditions of the inheritance and your trustee can distribute money without having to worry about facing a judge.

Not sure if you need a trust? A financial advisor or estate attorney can take a look at your finances and assets to see if you need one. Even if you do decide to set up a trust, Lester recommends always having a will as a backup.

What's a Power of Attorney (POA) and Why You Need One NOW!

When putting together your will, you should also think about who you want to make medical and financial decisions for you in case you're not able to make decisions for yourself while you're still alive. A power of attorney (or POA) is someone who acts on your behalf.

A medical power of attorney makes decisions about your health and a durable financial power of attorney can make decisions regarding your finances. Everyone over 18 should have POAs in place just in case something happens. To establish a power of attorney, you can also fill out a template using an online legal service like eForms.com or LegalZoom.com or you can file documents with an attorney. I recommend an attorney, but have also used online services for legal documents.

YOUNG ADULTS 18 – 25 NEED A POA—ASAP!

I consider myself pretty savvy in all things money, but I came up short when it came to making sure our kids who had graduated high school had a medical and financial POA. We still think of them as our kids once they turn 18 and often they still live with us. But if anything were to happen and they could not advocate for themselves, once they are 18, you have no parental rights to make medical decisions or access their finances.

This was an eye-opener for me after meeting with Attorney Lester and I hope it is for you too. Get a POA for your kids who are at home, on their own or in college as soon as possible.

Where Can You Find a Reputable Attorney?

While there are many financial steps you can DIY—like starting a budget and coming up with a debt payoff plan—when securing your family's future, there are times when it's best to pick up the phone and call in the professionals. Remember, writing up will, trust or power of attorney documents are key in deciding how to pass on your legacy, so you want to make sure it's done right!

To find a reputable attorney, try reaching out to family and friends for referrals. You can also search LinkedIn for attorneys in your area. Before hiring someone, interview them, and look them up in your state's attorney database to double-check that their license is in good standing.

Ugh, It's so Expensive!

Okay, I know, you are thinking you may not have the money. Guess, what, you save for it. Yes, you add it to your financial plan as a priority. Get one item at a time—start with a medical and a financial POA since it's a little cheaper. You can normally get both documents done for under $00 combined. Then get your Will done the following month for $250+/-. See, there's nothing like a plan to make it happen.

Reach out to your employer. My husband's job covered some of the expenses for us and that saved a lot of money. We had no idea until he called to ask. I shared this with a client, and she found out that it was a covered perk at her job as well. You may have the benefit at work and don't know it as well.

A word about online legal resources

Yes, there are online legal companies you can use as well. As a money expert, I did this with my first will years ago. But guess what, there wasn't anyone to explain all the important details to me. It's so much more than just 'creating a will'…or POA, etc. When my husband and I sat down with Attorney Lester once we got married, I walked away mind blown with how much I didn't know about the process. I was beyond grateful for her guidance, so yes, I'm a believer in DIY'ing when you can, but in this case, the assistance of a good estate lawyer was priceless.

 DO THIS ACTION STEPS
How to Secure Your Financial Future with a Will and POA

Setting up a will and POA can involve a decent amount of paperwork. There may be several phone calls and emails back and forth between you and your attorney, but don't get discouraged! Going through the steps to put a plan in place is worth the peace of mind.

1. **Write down your assets.** Think about the money you have and the things you own, including savings, property, and other valuables.

2. **Decide your beneficiaries.** Figure out how you'll split up your assets keeping in mind that you can change your will if you change your mind.

3. **Choose your executor.** Pick someone to handle your affairs after you pass away. This needs to be someone who you trust and who's capable of handling the probate process.

4. **Contact your employer.** Ask if they offer will or POA services for you, your spouse, and your children.

5. **Contact three attorneys for quotes.** Interview attorneys and compare options. If you decide not to hire an attorney, you can find online will templates at LegalZoom, Rocket Lawyer, TotalLegal, or US LegalWills. If you decide to use an online template or service, be sure to read state laws to ensure your will template is state compliant.

6. **Choose your POA and draft your POA documents.** Everyone over 18 needs a POA right away. POA documents may be part of your attorney's estate planning package. If not, you can find POA documents online at websites like eForms.com or legalzoom.com or you may find templates on your state's court website.

7. **Speak with your financial planner or attorney about a trust.** If you own property in multiple states or have many assets to pass on, consider talking with an attorney about establishing a trust.

 SAY THIS: #MONEYCHAT MANTRAS

" *Estate planning isn't scary*

" *I will ensure my Will, POA and estate documents are in place, this year*

YOUR NEXT STEPS

The #MoneyChat Challenge

WHENEVER MY DAUGHTERS WERE FACING a challenge growing up, I would tell them to 'boss up'—lift your head, square your shoulders, put your game face on and go get 'em. I'm saying that to you now too. BOSS UP. You've read the book, now I challenge you to put the principles to action so you can be successful financially.

What would it feel like if all your bills were paid each month? What would it feel like if you were able to completely pay off one of your larger debts? How wonderful would it be to take a dream vacation and pay cash. Shoot, what kind of relief would it be to get through holiday gifts without using credit cards? I think you get the picture.

Don't roll your eyes at me, I know everyone's situation is different, but you have to get started to make progress. I have no doubt that you will need to adjust as you go along. So let's give it 30 Days! Check out the #MoneyChat Challenge info below!

#MONEYCHAT CHALLENGE

**I challenge you to seriously focus on Rockin' your #MoneyChat
over the next 30 days with the steps below:**

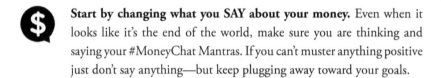

Start by changing what you SAY about your money. Even when it looks like it's the end of the world, make sure you are thinking and saying your #MoneyChat Mantras. If you can't muster anything positive just don't say anything—but keep plugging away toward your goals.

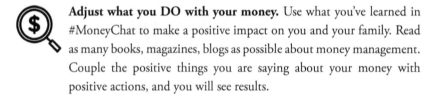

Adjust what you DO with your money. Use what you've learned in #MoneyChat to make a positive impact on you and your family. Read as many books, magazines, blogs as possible about money management. Couple the positive things you are saying about your money with positive actions, and you will see results.

Pay it Forward. Share what you have learned with others. I began learning how to properly manage money in my mid-twenties and I told everyone around me what I was learning. Some did get sick of me, but others were grateful to hear from someone they knew had been in the same boat as they were.

Share this Link. dorethiakelly.com/moneychatbook—don't keep all this #MoneyChat goodness to yourself. Share it with family and friends so they can get access to all the free financial bonuses. I would love to 'meet' them and join their journey to financial freedom!

Update Me! If you are game, drop me a line at hey@dorethiakelly.com with **I ACCEPT** so I can celebrate with you, offer encouragement or answer questions! Let me know your progress along the way—I am your coach and cheerleader!

HERE'S TO ROCKIN' YOUR #MONEYCHAT!

The #MoneyChat Book Summary

DO YOU WANT TO SHARE with family and friends how this book is helping you get your financial life together? Here's a book summary and an overview of each chapter.

Visit: #MoneyChat Hub: **dorethiakelly.com/moneychathub.** Access a download of the summary along with all the extra templates and tools to empower you financially that are mentioned throughout the book.

#MoneyChat Book Page: **dorethiakelly.com/moneychatbook.** Get your own copy of the book and special bonuses created for purchasers only.

What is *#MoneyChat*?

#MoneyChat is a personal finance guide that teaches you step-by-step how to manage your money so you can build a financially secure future.

Dorethia Kelly pulls from personal experience, advice from experts, and client success stories to share lessons and strategies that can change your financial life.

What *#MoneyChat* Covers in More Detail

If you dread looking at your bank account balance or wish you had a financial plan, *#MoneyChat* is the answer you've been looking for.

Dorethia Kelly's no-fluff guide gets down and dirty to explain financial concepts, everything from how life insurance works and how to plan for retirement to the basics of crypto investing. By the end of the book, you'll have a financial plan that will help you build savings, crush debt, and grow your net worth.

No financial topic is off-limits—she discusses the dangers of gambling, the risks of using payday loans, and how to avoid getting on the IRS's bad side. Dorethia's "big sister" approach to storytelling is bolstered by examples, resources, and guidance, making it a must-read for anyone who needs help taking their finances to the next level.

Section 1: Getting Out of the Hole

The first section of *#MoneyChat* is about addressing your money struggles. Dorethia offers solutions for challenging financial situations, such as managing high debt balances, dealing with student loans, and owing money to the IRS.

Chapter 1: Don't Manage Your Debt—Get Rid of It!

Debt is a four-letter word that keeps many people up at night. Making payments on revolving debt year in and year out can hold you back from reaching other financial goals. Dorethia kicks off chapter 1 of *#MoneyChat* by explaining how to get rid of debt once and for all using strategies she's seen work time and time again.

Chapter 2: Crush Your Student Loan Debt

If you're overwhelmed by your student loan balance, you're not alone— Americans hold over $1 trillion in student loan debt. In chapter 2 of *#MoneyChat*, Dorethia discusses ways to manage federal and private student loans. You'll learn how deferment, forbearance, and income-driven repayment works. Plus, you'll learn situations where your loans can be forgiven or discharged.

Chapter 3: It CAN Wait Until Payday! Cash Advance Loans

You've probably seen payday loan and cash advance advertisements on storefronts and online. Are they ever a good idea? In most cases, no. In chapter 3 of *#MoneyChat*, Dorethia discusses the dangers of payday loans and alternatives to consider if you need to borrow money to bridge a financial gap.

Chapter 4: IRS—Uncle Sam is Not Playing With You!

It can be pretty terrifying when you get a letter from Uncle Sam saying you owe money. The IRS has the power to garnish your wages and take your property if you don't pay a tax bill. Chapter 4 of *#MoneyChat* discusses scenarios where you could end up owing taxes so you can proactively avoid them. If you owe money, Dorethia explains how to settle debt so you can get Uncle Sam off your back.

Chapter 5: Gambling on Your Future

Gambling is an addiction that plagues people of all races and backgrounds. In chapter 5 of *#MoneyChat,* Dorethia illustrates how gambling can wreak havoc on your finances with stories from people who had a gambling habit that spiraled out of control. You'll learn the difference between recreational gambling and compulsive behavior. Plus, Dorethia includes resources you can turn to if gambling is negatively impacting your life and finances.

Section 2: Getting on Solid Ground

The second section of *#MoneyChat* is about establishing a solid foundation. Dorethia teaches how to set up a monthly budget, how to beef up your emergency savings, and how to build credit.

Chapter 6: Get Your Money Right!

Building a solid financial foundation starts with addressing your money mindset and creating a budget. You get a step-by-step process for doing both in Chapter 6 of *#MoneyChat.* Dorethia also discusses the importance of regular budget checkups and the benefit of choosing someone—a spouse, friend, relative, or a financial coach—to hold you accountable.

Chapter 7: The Infamous Emergency Fund

You've probably heard that you need an emergency savings account, but *why* and *how* do you start one? What if money is already tight and you can't see a way to squeeze out another dollar? In chapter 7 of *#MoneyChat*, Dorethia answers these questions, and you'll find out the best place to stash your cash.

Chapter 8: Why Good Credit Matters

If your credit score could use a bit of work, you don't want to miss chapter 8 of *#MoneyChat*. In it, Dorethia demystifies how credit works and explains how your FICO Score is calculated. You'll learn ways to build credit and what you need to know about credit repair companies before hiring one.

Section 3: Getting on Solid Ground

After you dig yourself out of a hole and establish a strong financial foundation, it's time to grow your dough and plan for the long term. In the third section of *#MoneyChat*, Dorethia covers investing, retirement, and college savings.

Chapter 9: Investing

Chapter 9 of *#MoneyChat* gives you an investing roadmap and teaches the importance of portfolio diversification. You'll get an overview of investment types and the types of investment accounts you can open.

Chapter 10: Digging Deeper

If you're intimidated by the words "dividend" or "bond," this chapter breaks down these terms (and many more) in black and white. Chapter 10 of *#MoneyChat* goes in-depth about how buying and selling stock works and explains what you need to know before investing in mutual funds.

Chapter 11: Retirement

In Chapter 11 of *#MoneyChat*, Dorethia takes a deep dive into the topic of retirement planning. She covers the different types of retirement accounts you can open. She also discusses factors to consider when deciding *when to save* and *how much to save* for the golden years.

Chapter 12: Retirement Investing for Young Adults—Manyell Akinfe-Reed

The earlier you plan for retirement, the better. In Chapter 12 of *#MoneyChat*, Dorethia, with the help of Manyell Akinfe-Reed, a financial expert in New York, covers how young people can stop leaving money on the table by taking advantage of employer match programs. You'll learn how to determine your risk tolerance and the four stages of retirement planning—accumulation, preservation, distribution, and fund transfer.

Chapter 13: Saving for College

The cost of college increases year after year. If you have a young child or one who's getting close to college age, you're probably wondering how you'll pay for it. In chapter 13 of *#MoneyChat*, Dorethia explores the different college savings options, such as the 529 College Savings Plan and Coverdell Education Savings Account (ESA). Other tips include how NOT to save for your kid's college education and eliminating any guilt from not being able to save.

Section 4: Securing Your Money

In the final section of *#MoneyChat*, Dorethia shares why and how to protect yourself with life insurance and how to leave a legacy with estate planning.

Chapter 14: Insurance

Securing life insurance is a way to cover your final expenses and transfer wealth so your family isn't financially burdened. Chapter 14 of *#MoneyChat* discusses what life insurance is, why you need it, and the different policies available.

Chapter 15: Wills, Trusts, & POAs

Everyone needs a will—even young adults. If you're not sure what should go into your will or estate plan, chapter 15 of *#MoneyChat* is jam-packed with information. Richelle Lester, an estate attorney, chimes in to explain how to draft a will, when you may need to set up a trust, and why you need a power of attorney (POA).

Make it Happen!

In #MoneyChat, Dorethia challenges you to change what you say and *think* about money over the next year. Words have power! Your words will manifest into action and results. Download your #MoneyChat Mantras (plus all the other amazing bonuses) from the hub and repeat daily.

Have you enjoyed the strategies you've learned so far to level up your finances? Want more? I've got you covered.

JOIN THE #MONEYCHAT FAM!!

You are never on this journey alone! Join a community of men and women who are leveling up their money without judgment or snark. No shame ever, all love …always.

When you join—get immediate access to:

- Monthly Q & A
- Monthly training on relevant topics that you choose!
- Downloads + resources
- Ask any question in the community and have it answered same day
- Community—we're in this together and here for each other
- Unlimited access to all recordings and trainings

Psst…everyone who buys the book qualifies for a special membership offer.

Head over to **moneychatbook.com** to claim yours!

#MONEYCHAT MASTERCLASS

What would if fee like to get your finances on track—not just for a month or two, but for a lifetime? Spend just a few short weeks with me and get realistic, no fluff strategies so you can:

- Pay off your debt and still enjoy the money you earn
- Increase your credit score—YOURSELF!
- Cover your fun/sport activities (or the kids') without strain
- Save for a home, vacation or dream purchase
- Create budget habits you can stick to this time
- Know where your money is going each pay
- Save more money and build real wealth

Well, that's exactly what you get in the #MoneyChat MasterClass. Real strategies to live financially free.

Yeah, you guessed it, if you are holding this book in your hands there's a special (aka crazy) offer waiting in your email you once you claim your bonuses at **moneychatbook.com**

About The Author

Dorethia R. Kelly, MBA, is a nationally-recognized and award-wining financial expert and coach, who enjoys empowering ordinary people to overcome their money hurdles without shame and guilt. She truly believes financial relief shouldn't come at the expense of your sanity and has helped thousands as a personal finance and business coach, author, and CEO of #MoneyChat®.

Known for her charismatic, no-nonsense personality, Dorethia empowers people to reach their financial, entrepreneurial, and career goals with her coaching, keynotes, and online courses. Dorethia's financial expertise has been featured on Black Enterprise, CNBC, U.S. News, USA Today, Experian, and more. Get her cutting-edge advice through her blog, courses, and book at **DorethiaKelly.com.**

How To
Contact Dorethia

If you are interested in personal finance or entrepreneurship Dorethia can help.

For more information about keynotes, speaking engagements or brand partnerships please contact Dorethia Kelly's team at:

EMAIL: speak@dorethiakelly.com

ONLINE: DorethiaKelly.com

Dorethia Kelly's #MoneyChat
607 Shelby St. #727
Detroit, MI 48226

Sign up for the #MoneyChat newsletter at **DorethiaKelly.com**

Remember you can get all the tools mentioned throughout the book here: dorethiakelly.com/moneychathub

Connect with Dorethia and say Hi!

facebook.com/groups/MoneyChatters

@dorethiakelly

@dorethiakelly